CGP

11+ Practice Paper
For Ages 8-9
Set A: Paper 1
For the CEM Test

Read the following:

Do not open this booklet or start the test until you are told to do so.

1. This test can be taken in either multiple-choice or write-in format.

2. If you are taking it as a multiple-choice test, you should mark your answer to each question in pencil on the separate answer sheet. Mark the correct box quickly and neatly using a horizontal line.

3. If you are taking it as a write-in test, you should write your answer to each question in pencil on the paper. Write your answer carefully in the space provided or, if there is a range of options, mark the correct box quickly and neatly using a horizontal line.

4. If you make a mistake, rub it out and mark your new answer clearly.

5. There are six sections in this test.

6. The time allowed for each section is given at the start of that section. You will have a total of 45 minutes to complete the timed sections of the test.

7. Each section includes examples showing you how to answer the questions. You may refer to these examples at any time as you work through the section.

8. Do as many questions as you can. For some questions you will be given a range of options — if you get stuck on one of these questions, choose the answer that you think is most likely to be correct, then move on to the next question. If you get stuck on a question for which no options are given, leave it and move on to the next question. If you have time at the end of the section, go back and have another go at the questions you could not answer.

9. You should do any rough working on a separate piece of paper.

Work carefully, but go as quickly as you can.

Exam Set ELY4PDE1 © CGP 2019

Section 1: Verbal Reasoning — Comprehension

Example Read these example questions. You may return to these examples at any time as you work through this section.

Wojtek the Warrior Bear

1   People have been introduced to many famous bears in the last century, including Paddington, Winnie-the-Pooh and Yogi Bear. However, one extraordinary bear who is seldom mentioned is Corporal Wojtek, who served in the Polish Army during World War Two. Born in Iran in 1942, Wojtek's mother died when he was just a cub.
5   Wojtek was discovered by an Iranian boy and later adopted by Polish soldiers.
   Wojtek, whose name in Polish roughly translates to 'Happy Warrior', travelled with the soldiers to various locations between Iran and Egypt. They continued to foster the bear, and Wojtek grew considerably in height and weight. Despite his size, Wojtek had a very gentle nature. He adored play-wrestling with the soldiers and
10   learnt to salute when greeted. The soldiers found Wojtek to be a welcome distraction from the war.

(A) According to the passage, which statement about Wojtek is true?
- A   He was born in Poland.
- B   He was discovered by Egyptian soldiers.
- ■ C   His mother died when he was young.
- D   He served in World War One.

(B) Why do you think the soldiers let Wojtek travel with them?
- A   They had extra food that needed eating.
- ■ B   He helped take their mind off the conflict.
- C   They wanted to improve their strength by wrestling him.
- D   They needed an extra soldier.

End of example questions

⚠ **Wait until you are told to go on** ⚠

You have 15 minutes to complete this section

There are 20 questions in this section

Read the passage carefully and then answer the questions that follow.

The History of Halloween

1 **Frightful Fun**
   With windows lit by glowing pumpkins and streets full of children dressed up as monsters, Halloween is considered by many to be the spookiest night of the year. While its origins can be found in an ancient festival, the Halloween we know today
5 is actually a combination of celebrations from numerous cultures and time periods. There have been lots of festivals throughout history that took place as the days got colder and winter approached. However, a lot of people believe that the celebration that became known as Halloween started as the ancient Celtic festival 'Samhain'.

Samhain
10 Around two-thousand years ago, groups of Celts* lived in the UK and Ireland. Each year on 31st October, they celebrated Samhain to mark the end of the harvest season and the beginning of winter. During Samhain, the Celts believed that the border between our world and the Otherworld (the realm of spirits) was easier to cross. As a result, on this night, these spirits were able to return to earth. It is
15 believed that the Celts may have sacrificed cattle and crops on large bonfires in order to please the spirits and gain their favour for the coming winter.
   Throughout history, other supernatural activities often took place on this night. Some of these involved predicting someone's future partner. It is thought that one of the ways this was done was by thinking of the name of a possible partner and
20 then choosing a nut to roast on the fire. It was believed that if the nut burned down to ash, it was a sign that the couple were meant to be married.

All Hallows' Day
   As Christian influence in Britain grew, Celtic traditions like Samhain began to fall out of favour. An example of this can be seen in the eighth century when
25 All Hallows' Day started to be celebrated on 1st November. All Hallows' Day is a Christian festival for honouring saints. As Samhain continued to lose popularity, it eventually became known as 'All Hallows' Eve' — meaning 'the day before All Hallows' Day'. Over time, this would change to be known simply as 'Halloween'.

Passage continues over the page

All Hallows' Day also brought about new traditions that remain in some form today.
30 For example, on All Hallows' Day, individuals would knock on doors to sing songs and beg for food or money. These individuals were called 'soulers' and were often children or the poor. People who answered their doors would give the individuals soul cakes (small cakes filled with spices and raisins). In return for these cakes, they asked the soulers to pray for the souls of their relatives. Over the years, the
35 tradition of souling eventually moved away from its Christian roots and evolved into the trick-or-treating that is often practised on Halloween today.

Halloween through the centuries
Apart from in Scotland and Ireland, Halloween's popularity in the British Isles dwindled throughout the 1600s as other festivities such as Guy Fawkes Night were
40 introduced. However, in the 1700s, many Europeans moved to North America, and it was across the Atlantic Ocean that Halloween started to take on its present-day form.
Initially, Halloween was only celebrated in some Southern United States, where people would dance and share ghost stories. However, Halloween's popularity in the United States increased in the nineteenth century when a large number of
45 Irish and Scottish immigrants** moved there. By the early 1900s, it would not have been surprising to see people dressing up in costumes, trick-or-treating or attending Halloween parties on the evening of October 31st.

Halloween in the present
In the United States, Halloween has continued to grow in popularity — costumed
50 street parades, terrifying horror films and houses covered with gruesome decorations are now a popular part of the festivities. Following this continued rise, Halloween in the UK has become significantly more popular. It has also become increasingly similar to the celebrations in the United States. The popularity of activities such as trick-or-treating and pumpkin carving has led to increased spending on Halloween.
55 In 2017, it was estimated that £25 million would be spent in Britain on pumpkin carving alone. As Halloween becomes larger and more spectacular, it's hard to imagine its simpler beginnings thousands of years ago.

*Celts — *the name that's been given to tribes who lived in Britain, Ireland and other parts of Europe during the Iron Age*

**immigrants — *people who come to a new country to live there*

Answer these questions about the text. You can refer back to the text if you need to. Pick the best answer and draw a line through the rectangle next to it.

1) According to the text, why is Halloween thought to be the "spookiest night of the year" (line 2)?

- A It takes place when the days are colder.
- B People wear scary costumes on Halloween.
- C Halloween is a mixture of different celebrations.
- D It has origins in an ancient festival.

2) What did the Celts believe the Otherworld was?

- A The home of otherworldly spirits
- B Another version of Earth
- C The other side of the world
- D A world in the centre of the planet

3) Why might the Celts have sacrificed cattle and crops?

- A They wanted to stop the spirits returning to Earth.
- B They wanted to create huge bonfires.
- C They wanted to predict marriages.
- D They wanted to make the spirits happy.

4) According to the text, which of the following activities took place on 31st October?

- A Marrying couples by a bonfire
- B Roasting nuts
- C Talking to spirits
- D Giving soul cakes

5) In the eighth century, which festival was celebrated the day after Samhain?

- A Guy Fawkes Night
- B All Hallows' Eve
- C Halloween
- D All Hallows' Day

Go to the next question ⇨

6 According to the text, why did Samhain become less popular in the eighth century?

- [ ] **A** All Hallows' Day was a more fun celebration
- [ ] **B** Celtic traditions weren't followed as much anymore
- [ ] **C** It became illegal to celebrate Samhain
- [ ] **D** Souling wasn't allowed during Samhain

7 Which of these statements is false?

- [ ] **A** Soul cakes contain spices and raisins.
- [ ] **B** Soulers asked people to pray for their souls on All Hallows' Day.
- [ ] **C** Soul cakes were given out to beggars on All Hallows' Day.
- [ ] **D** Children would go knocking on doors on All Hallows' Day.

8 According to the text, which activity did trick-or-treating develop from?

- [ ] **A** Costumed street parades
- [ ] **B** Sharing ghost stories
- [ ] **C** Souling
- [ ] **D** Sacrificing crops

9 According to the text, which of the following started to be celebrated around the same time that Halloween became less popular in some parts of the British Isles?

- [ ] **A** Guy Fawkes Night
- [ ] **B** Christmas
- [ ] **C** Easter
- [ ] **D** All Hallows' Eve

10 Where was Halloween first celebrated in the United States?

- [ ] **A** The Atlantic Ocean
- [ ] **B** Eastern States
- [ ] **C** New York
- [ ] **D** Southern States

11 Why did Halloween's popularity increase in the US during the 1800s?

- [ ] **A** People wanted to join in with the Halloween dances.
- [ ] **B** People in Southern US states spread Halloween traditions to the north.
- [ ] **C** People started to enjoy ghost stories more.
- [ ] **D** People from Ireland and Scotland took their Halloween traditions with them when they moved there.

12 According to the text, which two of the following are part of modern-day Halloween celebrations?

1) Trick-or-treating
2) Keeping evil spirits away
3) Decorating houses
4) Communicating with the dead

☐ A   1 and 2
☐ B   1 and 3
☐ C   2 and 3
☐ D   3 and 4

13 According to the text, roughly how much money was expected to be spent on pumpkin carving in Britain in 2017?

☐ A   £1 million
☐ B   £2.5 million
☐ C   £25 million
☐ D   £125 million

14 Which of the following is not mentioned in the text?

☐ A   The type of film that is popular during Halloween.
☐ B   That there are similarities between Halloween in the US and Britain.
☐ C   The amount of money spent on Halloween costumes.
☐ D   The Halloween activities Americans enjoyed in the 1900s.

15 What do lines 56-57 tell you about the writer's opinion of Halloween?

☐ A   They don't like people who wear costumes on Halloween.
☐ B   They think Halloween has changed a lot.
☐ C   They think pumpkins are too expensive.
☐ D   They think Halloween was better when it was simpler.

Go to the next question ⇨

16 What does the word "numerous" (line 5) mean?
- A Various
- B Enormous
- C Popular
- D Never-ending

17 What does the phrase "brought about new traditions" (line 29) mean?
- A People paid to take part in new events.
- B New traditions developed.
- C Everyone enjoyed the new traditions.
- D The new traditions raised money for charity.

18 What is meant by the word "evolved" (line 35)?
- A Changed
- B Expanded
- C Merged
- D Succeeded

19 What does the word "dwindled" (line 39) mean?
- A Shortened
- B Simplified
- C Declined
- D Finished

20 What does the word "gruesome" (line 50) mean?
- A Beautiful
- B Fragile
- C Expensive
- D Horrible

Stop — you may check your answers in this section only

BLANK PAGE

Section 2: Verbal Reasoning — Synonyms

Example Read this example question. You may return to this example at any time as you work through this section.

Choose the word which means the same, or nearly the same, as the word on the left.

(A) **small**   tiny   strong   large   soft

⚠ Wait until you are told to go on ⚠

You have 5 minutes to complete this section

There are 16 questions in this section

Choose the word which means the same, or nearly the same, as the word on the left.

(1) **drink**   gobble   pour   drench   sip

(2) **fit**   activity   healthy   practical   trained

(3) **groan**   whisper   shout   complain   mumble

(4) **complete**   finish   perfect   ending   improved

(5) **famous**   rich   celebrated   pretty   happy

(6) **delicious**   sweet   enjoyable   rich   tasty

7	**conversation**	argument ☐	agreement ☐	speech ☐	chat ☐
8	**steal**	borrow ☐	loot ☐	deceive ☐	crime ☐
9	**break**	relax ☐	shatter ☐	stretch ☐	twist ☐
10	**calm**	pleasant ☐	peaceful ☐	beautiful ☐	delightful ☐
11	**illness**	injury ☐	sickness ☐	trouble ☐	health ☐
12	**grasp**	tighten ☐	catch ☐	clutch ☐	obtain ☐
13	**close**	shut ☐	tighten ☐	push ☐	unlock ☐
14	**pupil**	teacher ☐	tutor ☐	child ☐	student ☐
15	**complex**	long ☐	complicated ☐	enormous ☐	simple ☐
16	**repair**	build ☐	arrange ☐	redesign ☐	fix ☐

Stop — you may check your answers in this section only

Section 3: Verbal Reasoning — Antonyms

Example Read this example question. You may return to this example at any time as you work through this section.

Complete the word on the right so that it means the opposite, or nearly the opposite, of the word on the left.

A) strong — w e a k

⚠ **Wait until you are told to go on** ⚠

⏱ **You have 5 minutes to complete this section** ⏱

There are 14 questions in this section

Complete the word on the right so that it means the opposite, or nearly the opposite, of the word on the left.

1) real — f _ _ e

2) flat — h _ _ l y

3) innocent — g _ _ _ t y

4) sold — _ o _ g _ t

5) arrive — _ e a _ _

6) answer — _ _ e t i _ n

7) lie — t r u t h

8) rotten — f r e s h

9) tidy — m e s s y

10) bent — s t r a i g h t

11) safety — d a n g e r

12) exit — e n t r a n c e

13) piece — w h o l e

14) accept — r e j e c t

Section 4: Verbal Reasoning — Related Words

Example — Read this example question. You may return to this example at any time as you work through this section.

The words in bold are related in some way. Mark the rectangle under the word that fits best with the words in bold.

(A) **blue green red yellow**   colour   pink   paint   write   art

⚠ Wait until you are told to go on ⚠

You have 5 minutes to complete this section

There are 15 questions in this section

The words in bold are related in some way. Mark the rectangle under the word that fits best with the words in bold.

(1) **cup trophy award ribbon**   win   medal   compete   achieve   first

(2) **English German Spanish Dutch**   language   place   France   lesson   Italian

(3) **Norwich Liverpool Bristol Leeds**   city   England   Oxford   town   capital

(4) **chilly cool frosty snowy**   icicle   freezing   blizzard   breeze   winter

(5) **orchestra singers band musicians**   music   choir   guitar   perform   song

(6) **fantastic terrific great grand**   delicious   rich   joyful   superb   best

#	Words	Options
7	spaghetti burger hotdog pizza	meal ☐ warm ☐ pie ☐ bread ☐ meat ☐
8	cod tuna carp salmon	fish ☐ frog ☐ water ☐ prey ☐ haddock ☐
9	knuckle palm finger nail	thumb ☐ muscle ☐ toe ☐ hand ☐ fist ☐
10	aquarium pen birdcage hutch	pet ☐ food ☐ animal ☐ catch ☐ coop ☐
11	vinegar relish mayonnaise gravy	jam ☐ mustard ☐ side ☐ wrap ☐ dinner ☐
12	Europe Asia Antarctica Oceania	Earth ☐ continent ☐ Britain ☐ land ☐ Africa ☐
13	joker jester fool comedian	funny ☐ king ☐ clown ☐ audience ☐ silly ☐
14	adventure trip quest voyage	hero ☐ story ☐ journey ☐ destination ☐ travelling ☐
15	century year week month	time ☐ calendar ☐ Monday ☐ noon ☐ decade ☐

Stop — you may check your answers in this section only

Section 5: Numerical Reasoning

Example — Read these example questions. You may return to these examples at any time as you work through this section.

A Fill in the missing number to make this calculation correct: 8 × [ ][5] = 40

B Which Roman numeral means 64?

LXV ☐   LXVI ☐   XLIV ☐   LXIV ■   XLVI ☐

⚠ **Wait until you are told to go on** ⚠

⏱ **You have 8 minutes to complete this section** ⏱

There are **16** questions in this section

1 A shop sells lemons in packs of 4.
Phyllis needs 24 lemons.
How many packs of lemons should Phyllis buy?

2 Five children each flipped a coin a different number of times.
The number of heads and tails each child got is shown in this table.

Name	Heads	Tails
Saleem	8	3
Natalie	3	2
Clive	6	9
Isla	7	5
Oscar	4	5

How many fewer times did Saleem flip the coin than Clive?

(3) What is one thousand four hundred and seventy-six in figures?

(4) Cleo shades a shape on a grid.
Each square has an area of 1 cm².

What is the area of Cleo's shape? ☐☐ cm²

(5) Emlyn measures two sides of a triangle and finds they have the same length.
Which of these can't be the type of triangle Emlyn measured?

equilateral   isosceles   scalene   right-angled
   ☐   ☐   ☐   ☐

(6) The pictogram shows the number of pins knocked down by three bowlers.

Name	Number of pins
Tiffany	🎳🎳🎳🎳(half)
Evan	🎳🎳🎳🎳🎳
Nilesh	🎳🎳🎳(half)

🎳 = 2 pins

How many more pins than Nilesh did Evan knock down?

Go to the next question

7 Which number is equal to two tenths and seven hundredths?

0.72 ☐   720 ☐   0.27 ☐   20.7 ☐   0.027 ☐

8 What is the largest number you can make using the digits 3, 8, 2 and 6?

9 The first six terms in a sequence are:

11   8   5   2   ?   −4

Which number goes in the box to complete the sequence?

−2 ☐   1 ☐   −3 ☐   0 ☐   −1 ☐

10 Latisha is having afternoon tea at the time shown on the clock.

What is this time in the 24-hour clock format?

11 The grid below shows three corners of a square.

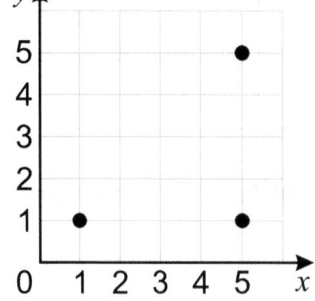

Give the coordinates of the missing corner of the square.

12) Ian weighs his prize-winning turnip.

How many grams does the turnip weigh? ☐☐☐☐☐ g

13) Depa fills ¾ of a glass with milk.
What is this fraction as a decimal?

0.25 ☐   0.8 ☐   0.75 ☐   0.5 ☐   0.34 ☐

14) Katya has £12. She spends £4.25 on a book.
Her grandad then gives her £2 pocket money.
How much money does Katya have now?

£☐☐.☐☐

15) Charles has collected 72 stamps.
Reuel has collected 3 times as many stamps as Charles.
How many stamps does Reuel have? ☐☐☐☐

16) Which of these numbers could replace the '?' in the sorting diagram?

9 ☐   6 ☐   16 ☐   4 ☐   18 ☐

multiples of 3: 21, 15
intersection: 24, ?
factors of 24: 2, 1, 8

Stop — you may check your answers in this section only

Section 6: Non-Verbal Reasoning

Example Read these example questions. You may return to these examples at any time as you work through this section.

A Work out which option would look like the figure on the left if it was reflected over the vertical line:

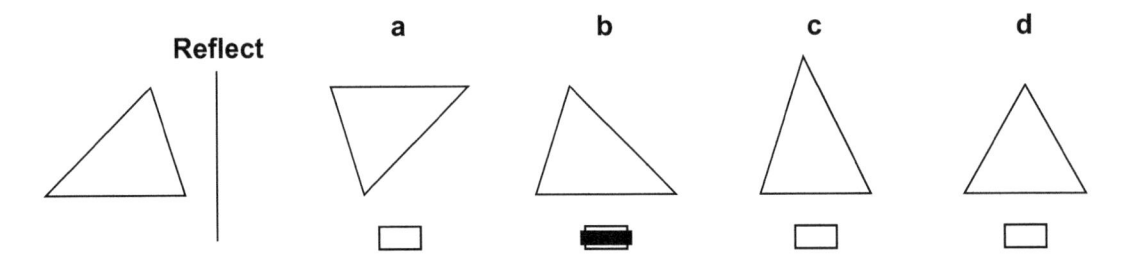

B Work out which of the four squares on the right best fits in place of the missing square in the series:

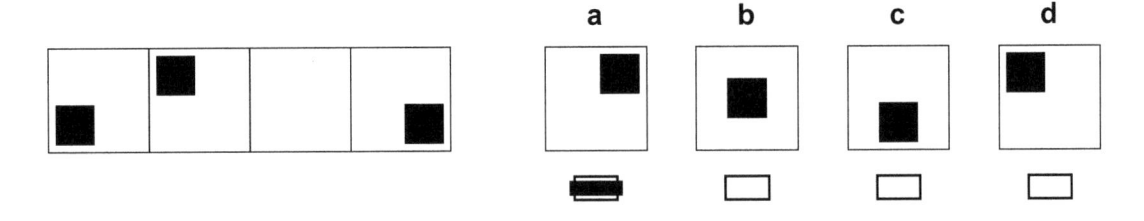

C Work out which option is most like the three figures on the left:

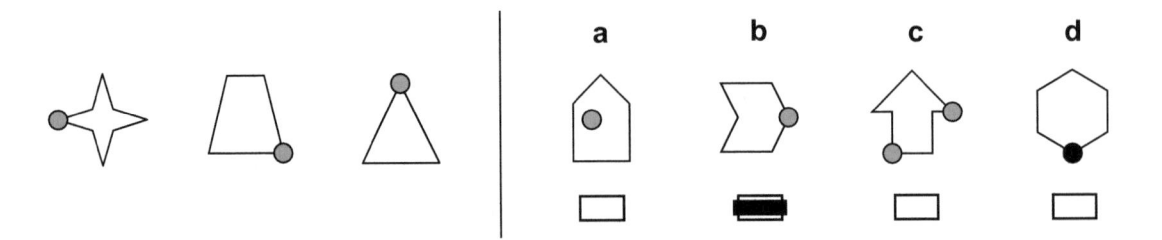

Wait until you are told to go on

You have 7 minutes to complete this section

There are 14 questions in this section

Work out which option would look like the figure on the left if it was reflected over the vertical line:

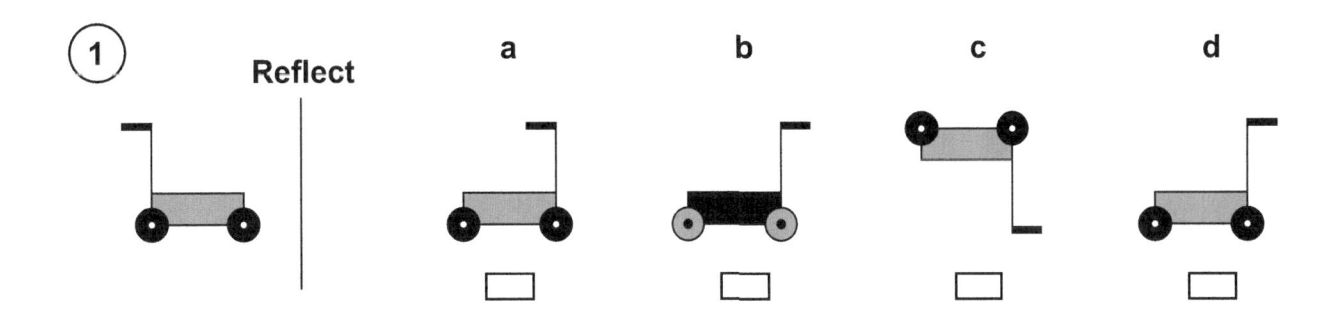

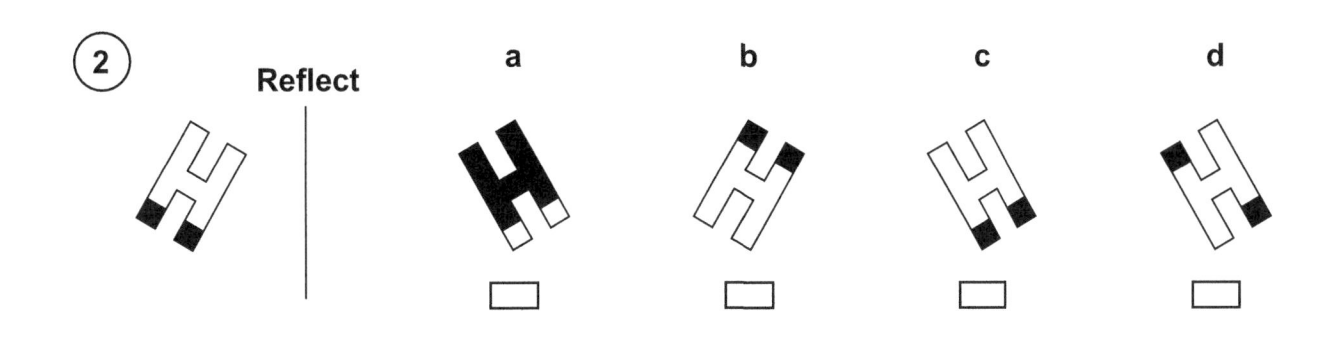

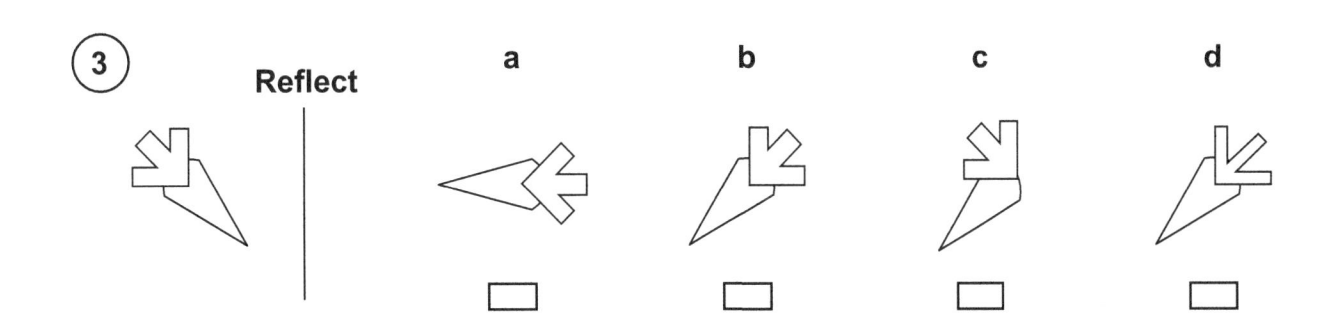

1 Reflect | a b c d

2 Reflect | a b c d

3 Reflect | a b c d

Go to the next question

4. Reflect

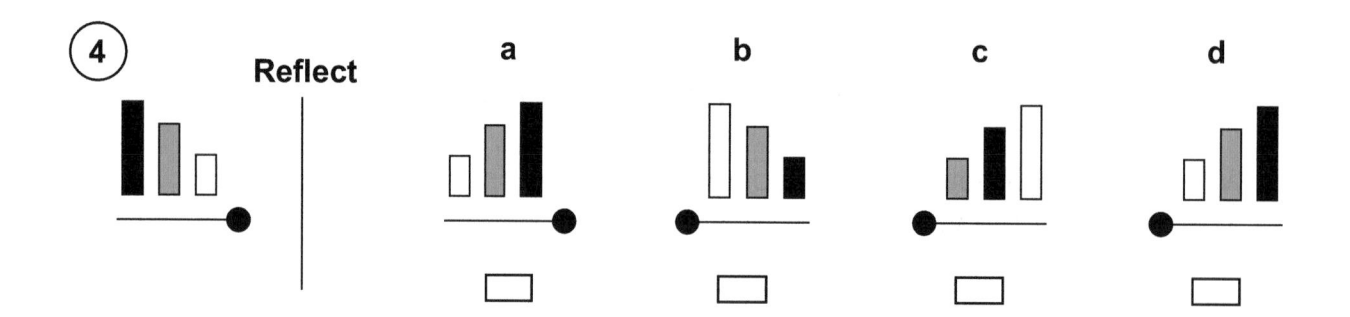

Work out which of the four squares on the right best fits in place of the missing square in the series:

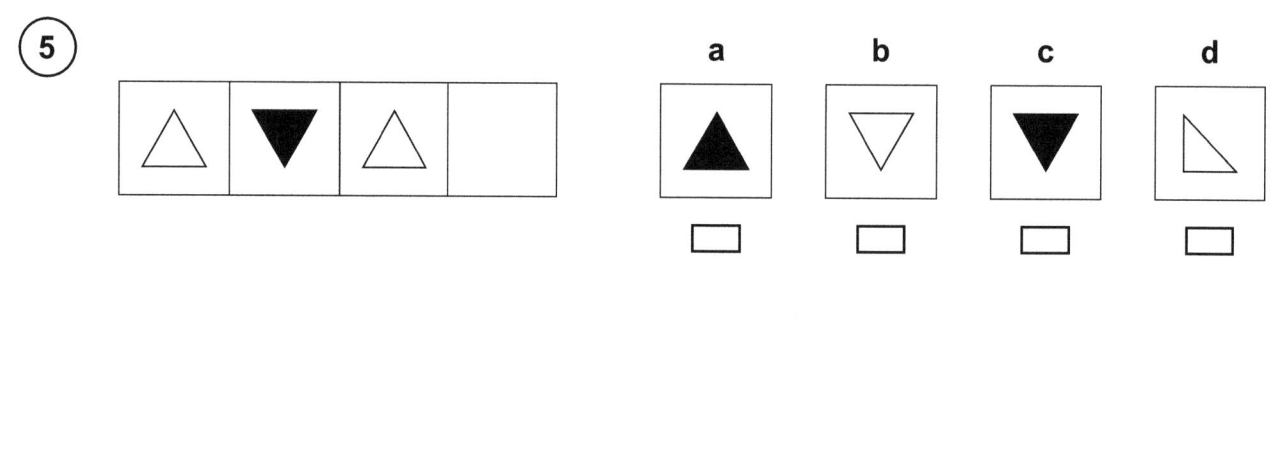

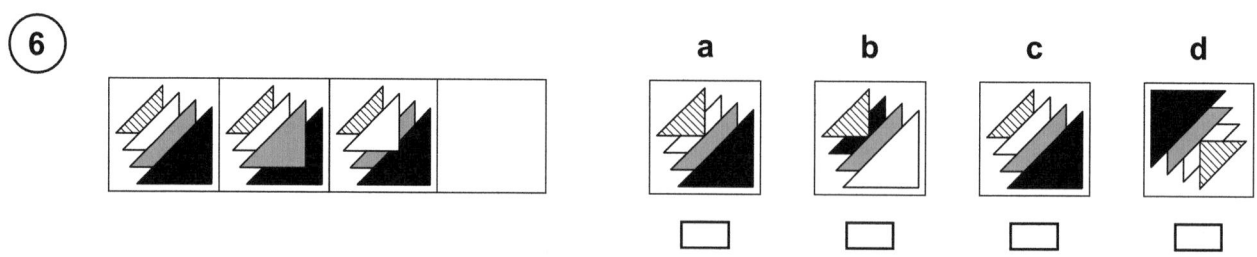

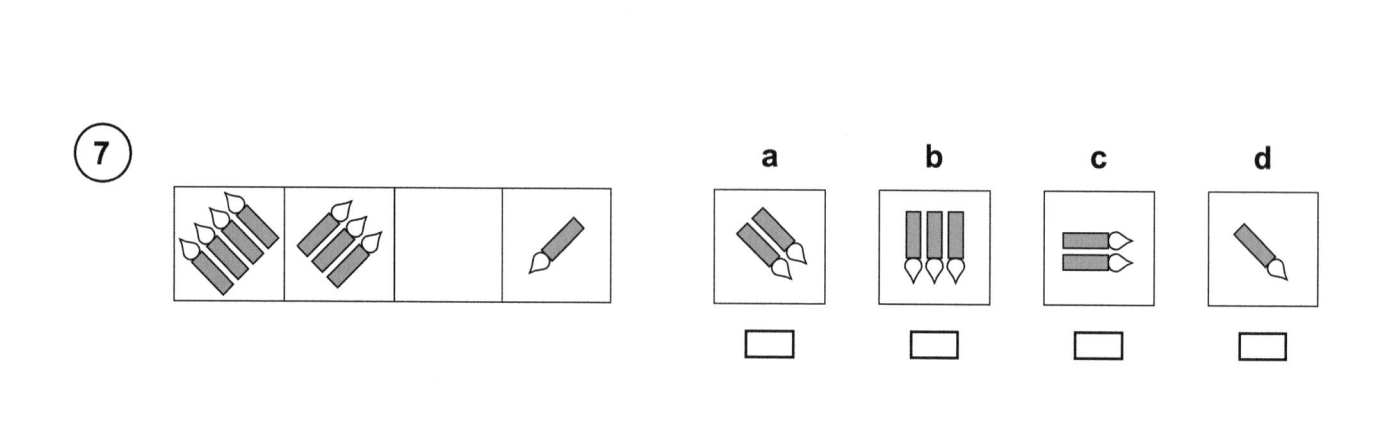

5.

6.

7.

8

9

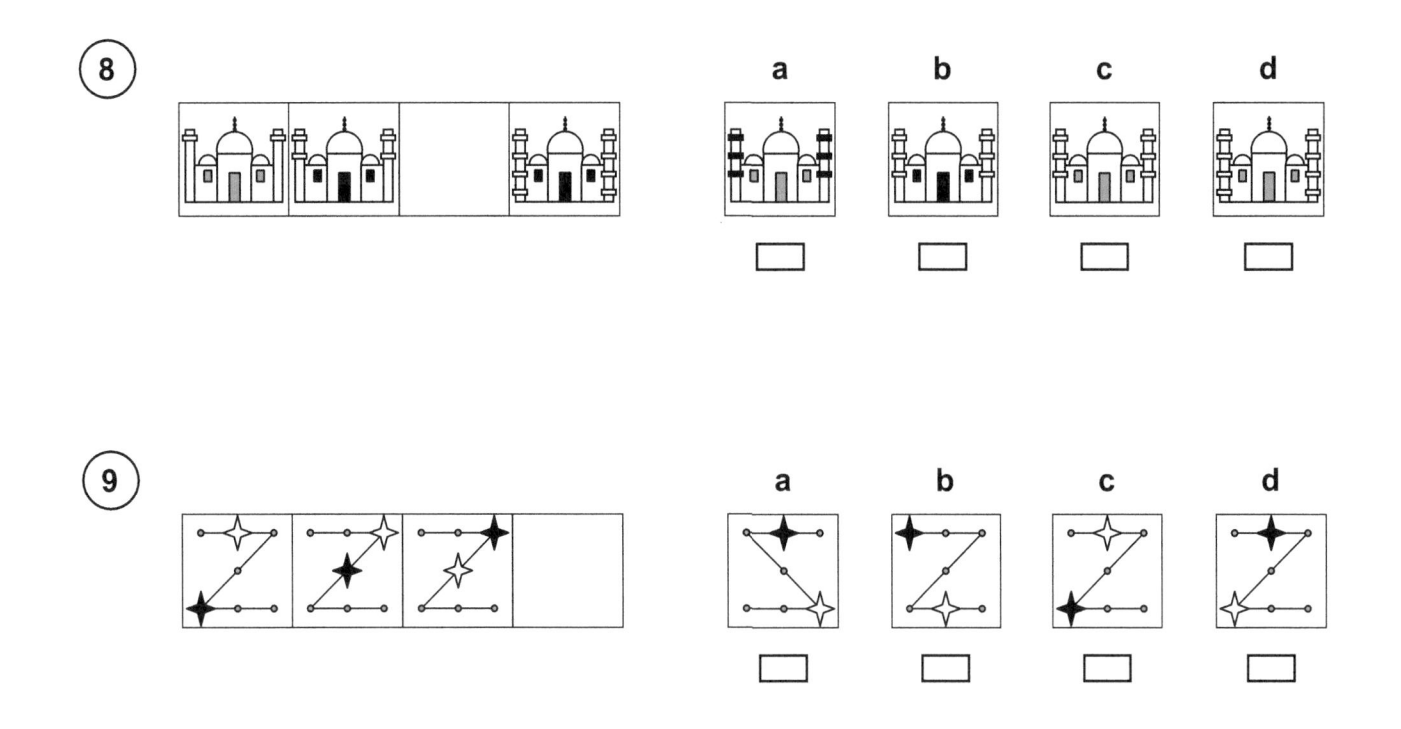

Work out which option is most like the three figures on the left:

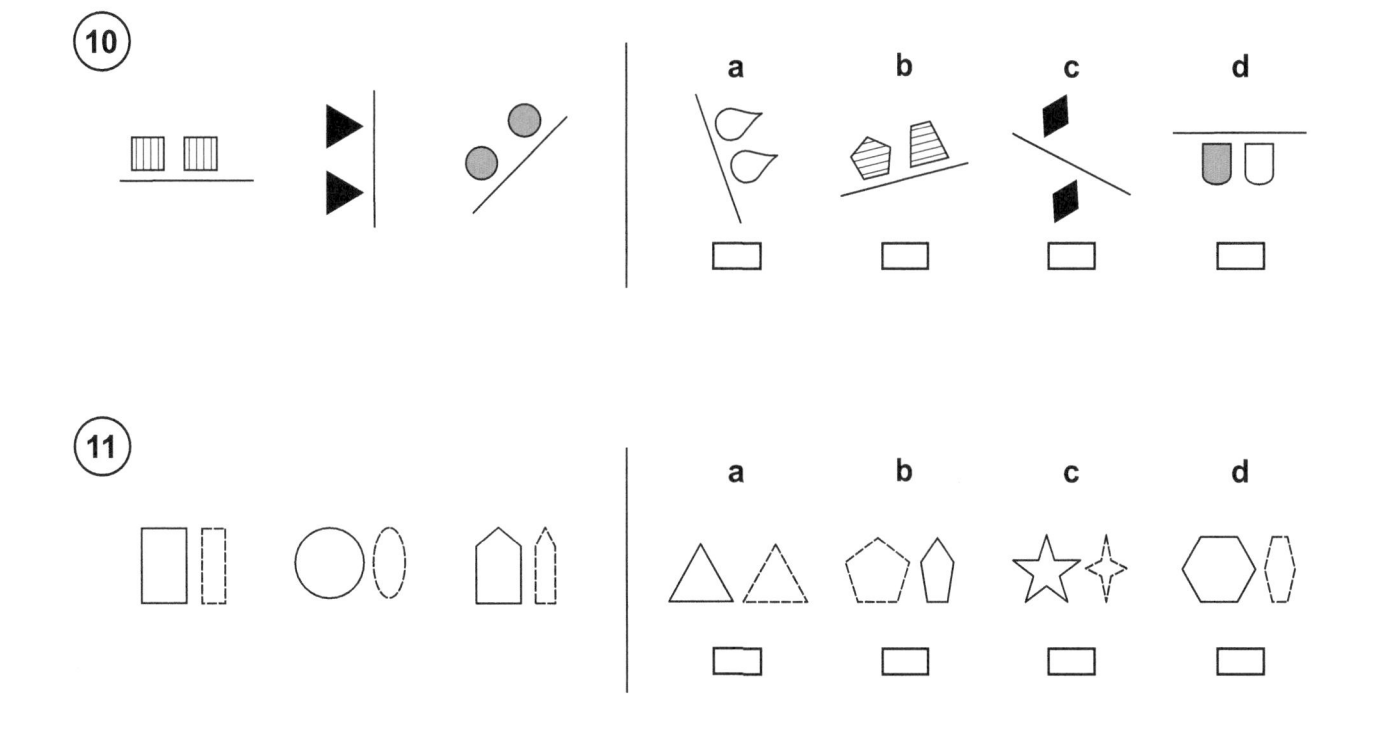

10

11

Go to the next question

12

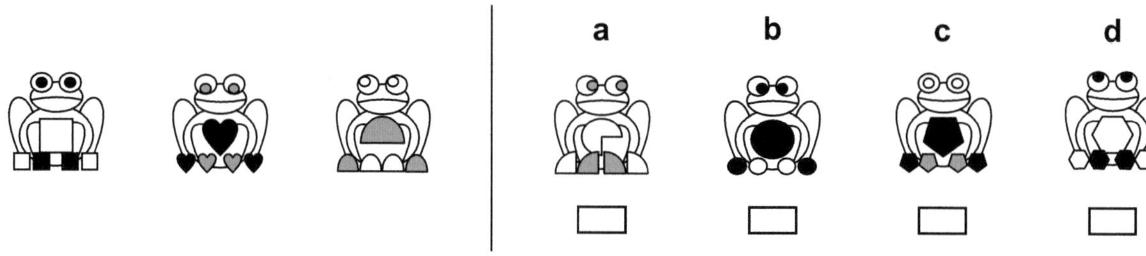

13

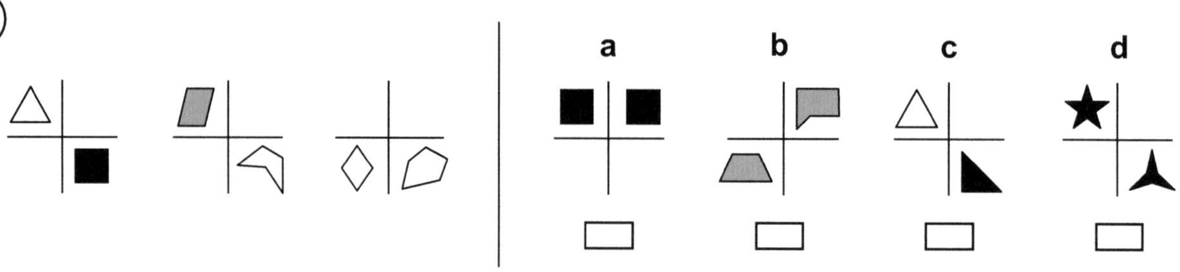

14

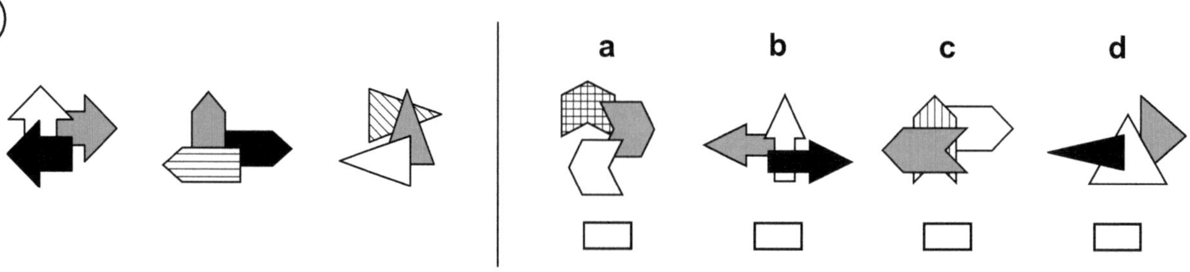

Stop — you may check your answers in this section only

CGP

11+ Practice Paper
For Ages 8-9
Set A: Paper 2
For the CEM Test

Read the following:

Do not open this booklet or start the test until you are told to do so.

1. This test can be taken in either multiple-choice or write-in format.

2. If you are taking it as a multiple-choice test, you should mark your answer to each question in pencil on the separate answer sheet. Mark the correct box quickly and neatly using a horizontal line.

3. If you are taking it as a write-in test, you should write your answer to each question in pencil on the paper. Write your answer carefully in the space provided or, if there is a range of options, mark the correct box quickly and neatly using a horizontal line.

4. If you make a mistake, rub it out and mark your new answer clearly.

5. There are three sections in this test.

6. The time allowed for each section is given at the start of that section. You will have a total of 45 minutes to complete the timed sections of the test.

7. Each section includes examples showing you how to answer the questions. You may refer to these examples at any time as you work through the section.

8. Do as many questions as you can. For some questions you will be given a range of options — if you get stuck on one of these questions, choose the answer that you think is most likely to be correct, then move on to the next question. If you get stuck on a question for which no options are given, leave it and move on to the next question. If you have time at the end of the section, go back and have another go at the questions you could not answer.

9. You should do any rough working on a separate piece of paper.

Work carefully, but go as quickly as you can.

Section 1: Numerical Reasoning

Example Read these example questions. You may return to these examples at any time as you work through this section.

A Mandy records how far a snail has moved every two minutes. She makes the graph below with her results.

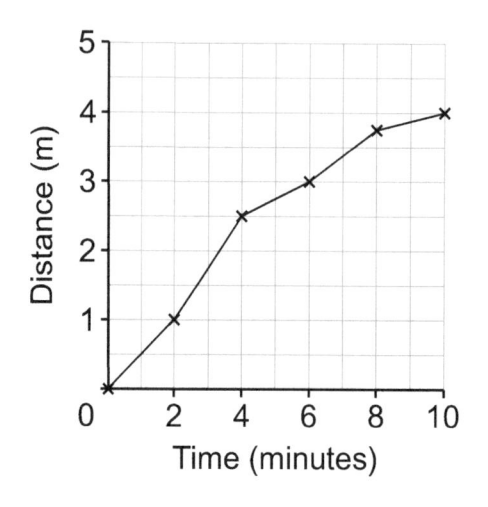

A1 How far did the snail move in the first 6 minutes?

☐ **3** m

A2 In what time period did the snail move the furthest?

0-2 minutes ☐   2-4 minutes ■   4-6 minutes ☐   6-8 minutes ☐   8-10 minutes ☐

⚠ **Wait until you are told to go on** ⚠

You have 25 minutes to complete this section

There are **13** multi-part questions in this section

1) Look at this shape.

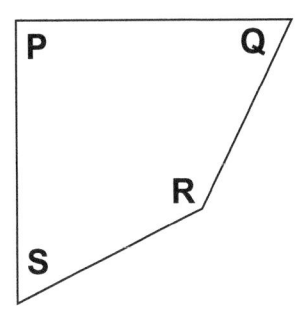

a) Which of the following statements is true?

☐ Angles Q and S are obtuse.
☐ Angles P and R are acute.
☐ Angle S is obtuse and angle R is acute.
☐ Angles Q and S are acute.
☐ All the angles are acute.

b) Which angle is a right angle?

P ☐   Q ☐   R ☐   S ☐

2) Sundeep and Carla are both growing their own chilli peppers.
A garden shop sells packs of 48 seeds.

a) Sundeep has one pack of seeds.
He shares the seeds equally between 12 pots.
How many seeds does he plant in each pot?

b) Carla wants to plant 150 seeds.
How many packs should she buy?

Go to the next question

3 Seth asks all the pupils in his class whether they are left-handed or right-handed. He records their responses in the tally chart below.

	Left-handed	Right-handed
Boys	IIII	IHI IHI II
Girls	I	IHI IHI III

a) How many pupils in Seth's class are right-handed?

b) What fraction of boys in Seth's class are left-handed?

$\frac{12}{16}$ $\frac{4}{12}$ $\frac{1}{14}$ $\frac{4}{16}$ $\frac{5}{12}$

4 Look at these numbers.

3, 18, 23, 32, 45, 57, 60, 99

a) Multiply together the first two odd numbers in the list.

b) Add together all the multiples of 5 in the list.

c) Which of these statements is true?

23 + 32 > 18 + 45   99 + 3 > 60 + 45   60 − 32 > 45 − 23

5) A school owns 912 books.
Half of the books are story books.

a) How many of the books are story books?

b) The school buys an extra 640 books, but donates 120 to charity.
How many books does the school own now?

6) This bar chart shows the number of cars of each colour in a car park.

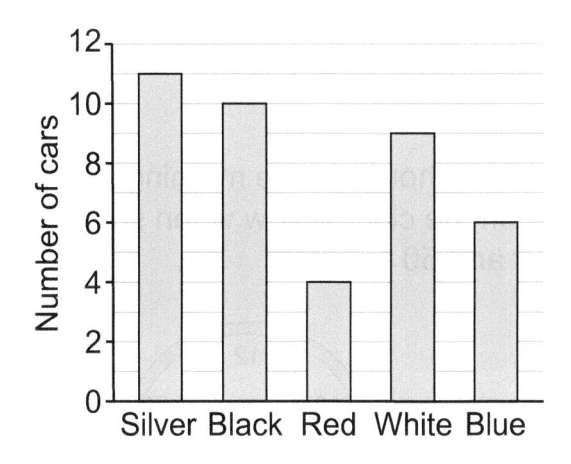

a) Janet's car is the third most common colour. What colour is Janet's car?

silver ☐   black ☐   red ☐   white ☐   blue ☐

b) How many cars in the car park are not blue?

c) Laurie washes all the red and black cars in the car park.
She charges £2.50 per car. How much money does she make in total?

£ ☐☐.☐☐

7 Look at these shapes.

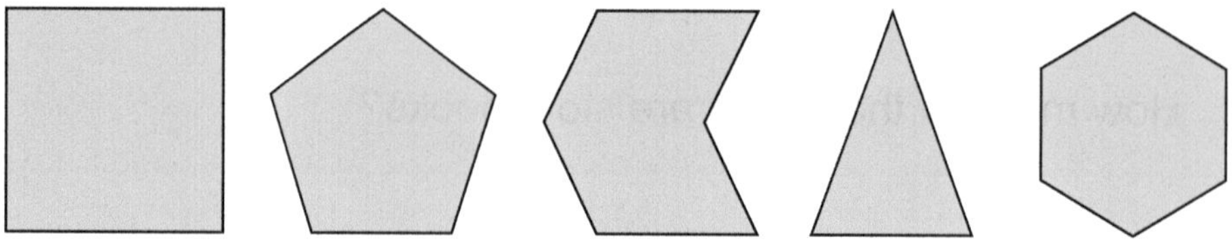

a) How many of the shapes are regular polygons?

☐

b) What fraction of the shapes are hexagons?

⅗ ☐   ⅕ ☐   ⅖ ☐   ½ ☐   ⅘ ☐

8 Rachel set off from her house in the morning and went running. She saw the time on the clock below when she left her house. She ran for 1 hour and 50 minutes.

a) What time did Rachel stop running?

8:05 pm ☐   7:55 am ☐   8:50 am ☐   8:55 am ☐   8:45 pm ☐

b) Rachel sprinted for ¹⁄₁₀ of the time she was running. How many minutes did she sprint for?

☐☐☐ minutes

9) Oti takes her £10 pocket money to a charity bookshop.
The prices at the shop are shown below.

> Paperbacks £1.25
> Hardbacks £2.50
> Magazines 10p

a) How many magazines could Oti buy?

b) Oti decides to buy one hardback and three paperbacks.
How much change does Oti get from a £10 note?

£ ☐☐.☐☐

10) Amelia draws the shape below and shades a fraction of it.

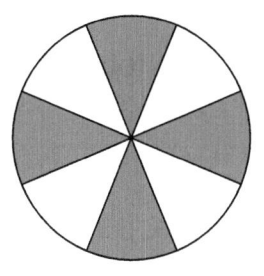

a) Which of the following shapes has the same fraction shaded?

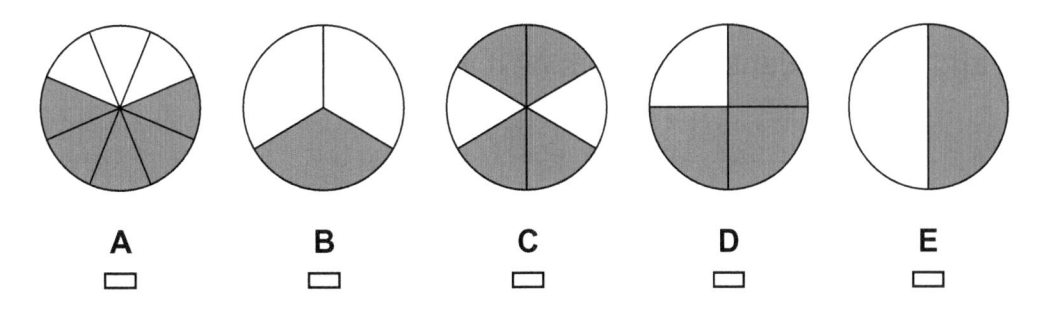

A B C D E

b) Amelia draws all the lines of symmetry on her shaded shape.
She starts by drawing a vertical line down the centre of the shape.
How many more lines of symmetry does she draw?

Go to the next question ➡

11) A new pupil at school asks how far away the park is.
Bryn estimates that the park is 1400 m from the school.
Hamish estimates that the park is 1.8 km from the school.

a) What is the difference between Bryn and Hamish's estimates?

☐☐☐☐ m

b) Bryn's estimate is the actual distance rounded to the nearest 100 m.
Which of the following could be the actual distance?

1460 m ☐   1349 m ☐   1451 m ☐   1328 m ☐   1439 m ☐

12) Farid buys 90 stickers from a craft shop. Each sticker costs 5p.

a) What do the stickers cost in total?

£☐☐.☐☐

b) $\frac{2}{3}$ of the stickers are purple. How many stickers are not purple?

☐☐

Farid sticks 4 identical stickers next to each other to make the shape below.

4 cm
3 cm

c) What is the perimeter of the shape Farid makes?

☐☐ cm

13) Five cousins measured their heights at a family party.
The table below shows their heights in metres.

Name	Height (m)
Bea	1.5
Aziz	1.2
Bill	1.19
Luke	1.65
Manon	1.47

a) What is the difference in height between the tallest and shortest cousin?

☐.☐☐ m

b) Manon's uncle is 36 cm taller than her.
How many centimetres tall is Manon's uncle?

☐☐☐ cm

c) Aziz's house is 10 metres high.
How many times will Aziz's height fit into the height of his house?

9 ☐   5 ☐   10 ☐   7 ☐   8 ☐

Stop — you may check your answers in this section only

Section 2: Verbal Reasoning — Cloze

Example Read these example questions. You may return to these examples at any time as you work through this section.

(A) The Solar System is made up of [p][l][a][n][e][t][s], asteroids and other

(B) bodies orbiting the Sun. Earth is the [t][h][i][r][d] planet from the Sun,

(C) after Mercury and [V][e][n][u][s].

Wait until you are told to go on

You have 6 minutes to complete this section

There are 16 questions in this section

The Paralympics are an international sporting competition for athletes

(1) with disabilities. The modern Paralympics [o][c][ ][ ][r] every four

years and take place shortly after the Olympic Games. The London 2012

(2) Paralympics were watched on [ ][e][l][ ][v][i][ ][ ][o][n] by roughly

3.8 billion people and featured over 4200 athletes from 164 countries.

(3) However, the Paralympics haven't always been such a [m][ ][ ][o][r]

(4) sporting event. While the Olympics have a long [ ][i][s][t][ ][r][ ]

beginning with the Ancient Greeks, the Paralympics are a more

(5) [r][e][ ][e][n][ ] development. Towards the end of World War Two,

a German doctor called Ludwig Guttmann began working with

(6) [s][ ][l][ ][ ][e][r][s] with spinal injuries in a special unit at

Stoke Mandeville Hospital in the UK. He began using a new method to

(7) treat his patients, which involved helping them to r e [ ] o v [ ] r

(8) by encouraging them to play sport. This proved so p o [ ] [ ] l [ ] r

that in 1948, Guttmann organised a competition for disabled athletes

which took place at the same time as the London Olympics. This event,

(9) which i [ ] v [ ] l [ ] e d an archery competition for athletes

(10) in w [ ] [ ] e l c [ ] a i [ ] s, was named the Stoke

Mandeville Games.

Following the success of the Stoke Mandeville Games, the International

(11) Stoke Mandeville Games were founded. These later [ ] e c [ ] m e

known as the Paralympics after the Games took place in Rome in 1960.

(12) The event has e x [ ] a n [ ] [ ] d over time so that athletes with a

(13) wider r a [ ] [ ] e of disabilities can compete. The number of sports

(14) included has also [ ] r [ ] w n, from eight in 1960 to twenty-two in 2016.

(15) The Paralympic Games play an [ ] m [ ] o r t [ ] n t role

in increasing public awareness of disabilities and in demonstrating the great

feats that people with disabilities are able to achieve. Every year, the

(16) Paralympics c o [ ] [ ] i n [ ] e to grow in popularity, and are now

considered by many to be an unmissable event in the sporting calendar.

Stop — you may check your answers in this section only

Section 3: Non-Verbal Reasoning

Example Read these example questions. You may return to these examples at any time as you work through this section.

A) Look at how the first two figures are changed, and then work out which option would look like the third figure if you changed it in the same way:

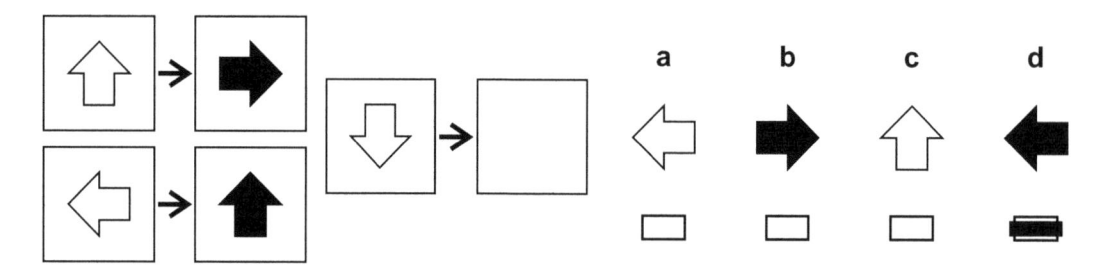

B) Work out which option is most like the two figures on the left:

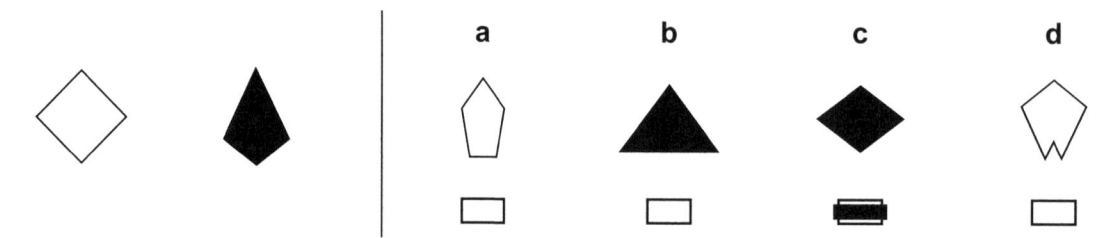

C) Work out which of the four squares on the right best fits in place of the missing square in the grid:

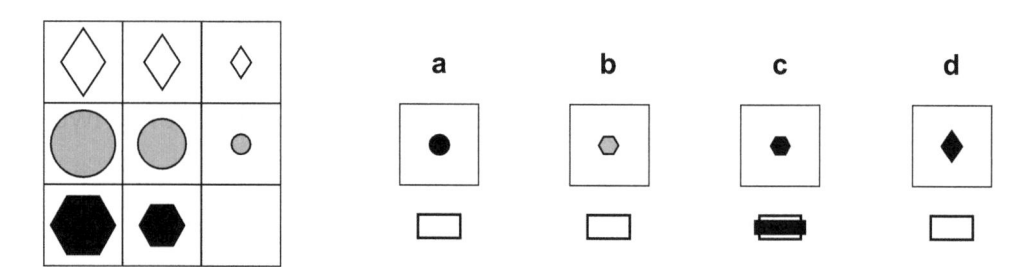

D) Work out which option would look like the figure on the left if it was rotated:

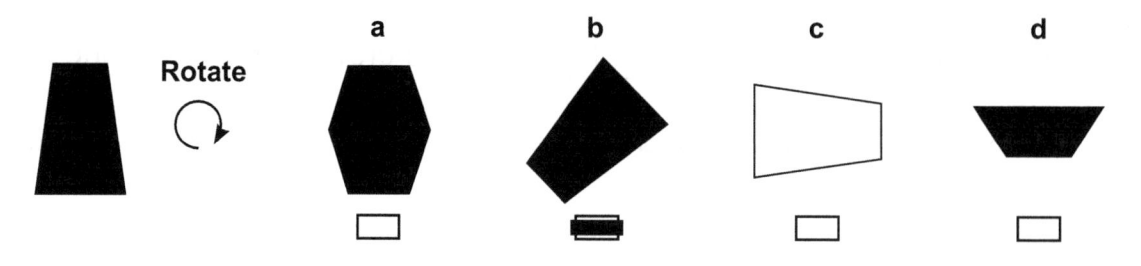

Wait until you are told to go on

E Find the figure in each row that is most unlike the other figures:

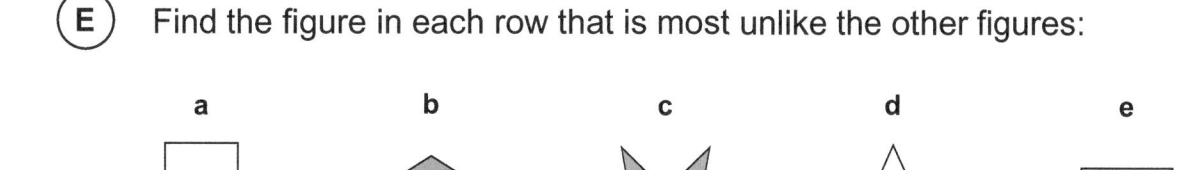

  a   b   c   d   e

You have 14 minutes to complete this section

There are 34 questions in this section

Look at how the first two figures are changed, and then work out which option would look like the third figure if you changed it in the same way:

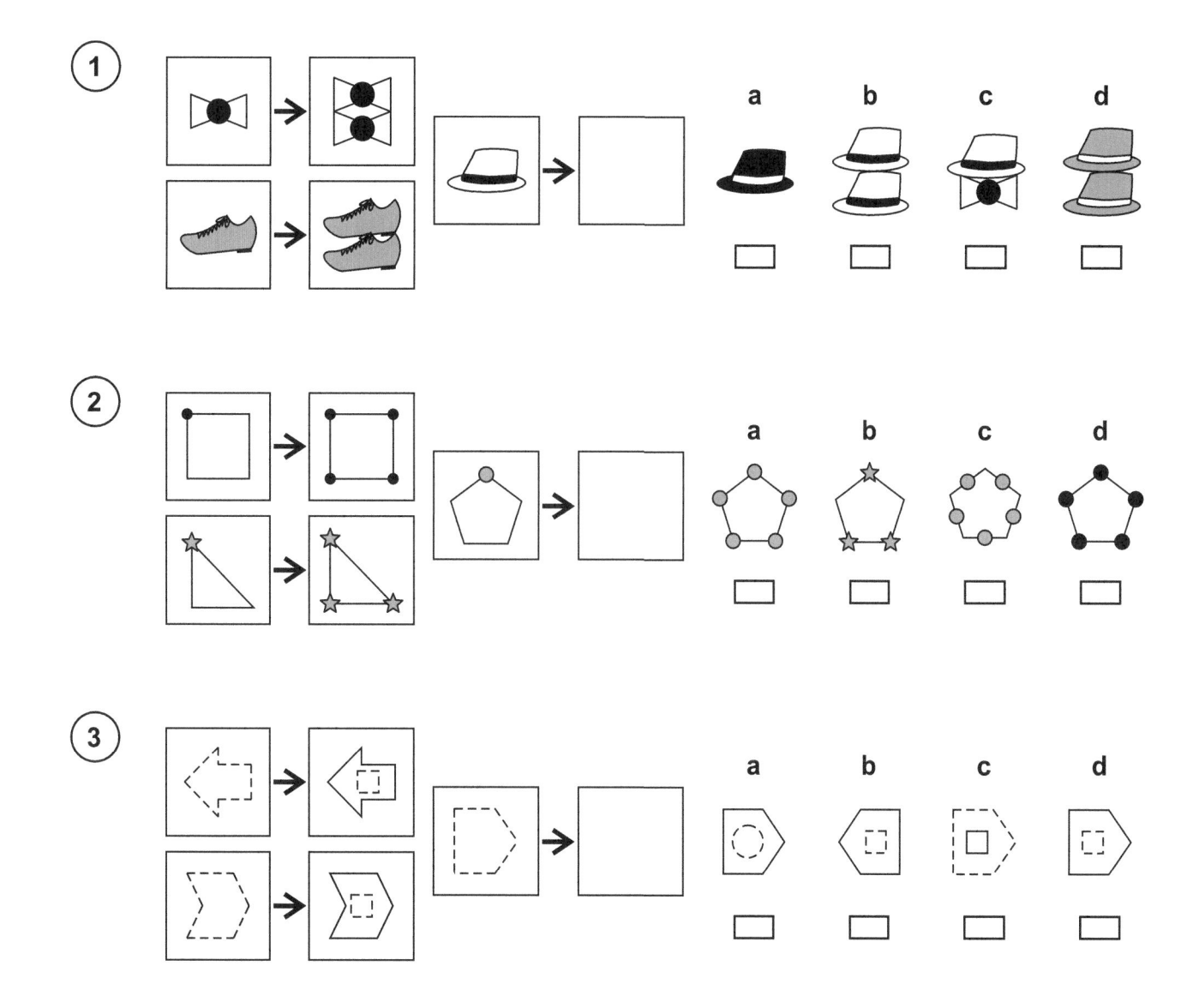

1

2

3

Go to the next question

4

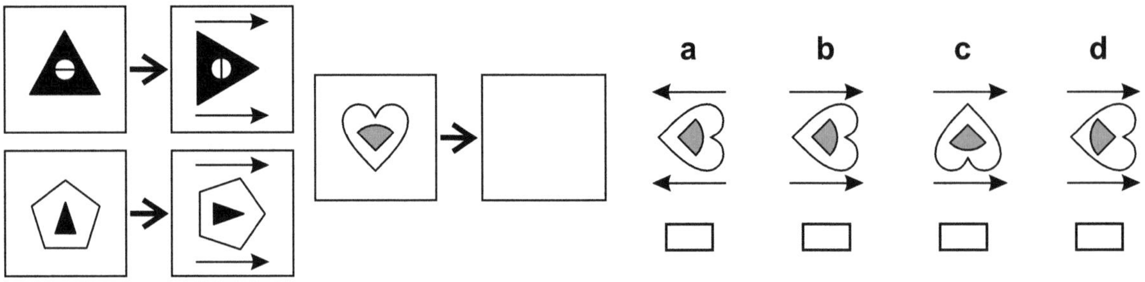

5

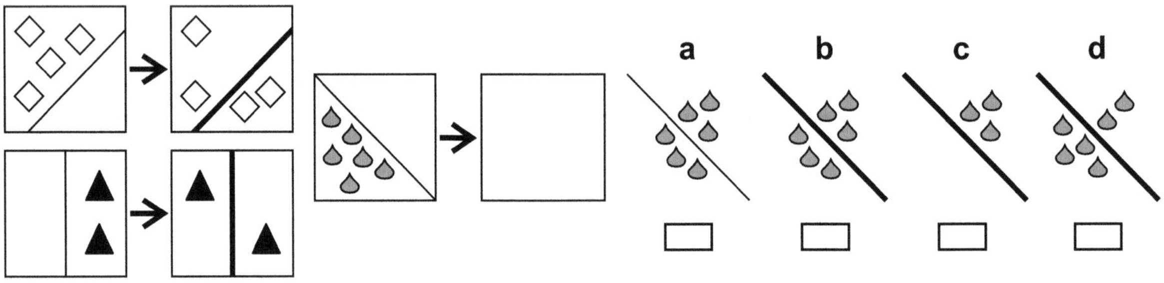

6

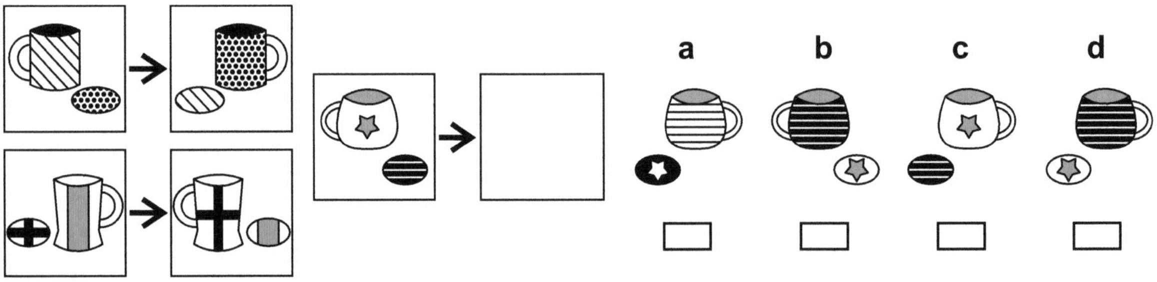

7

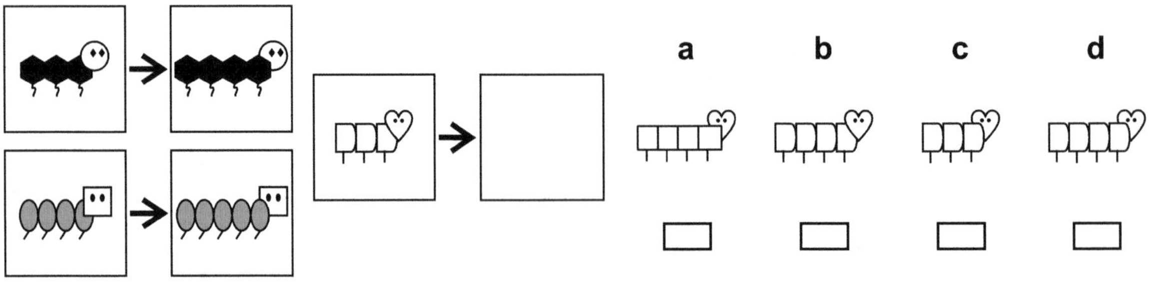

Work out which option is most like the two figures on the left:

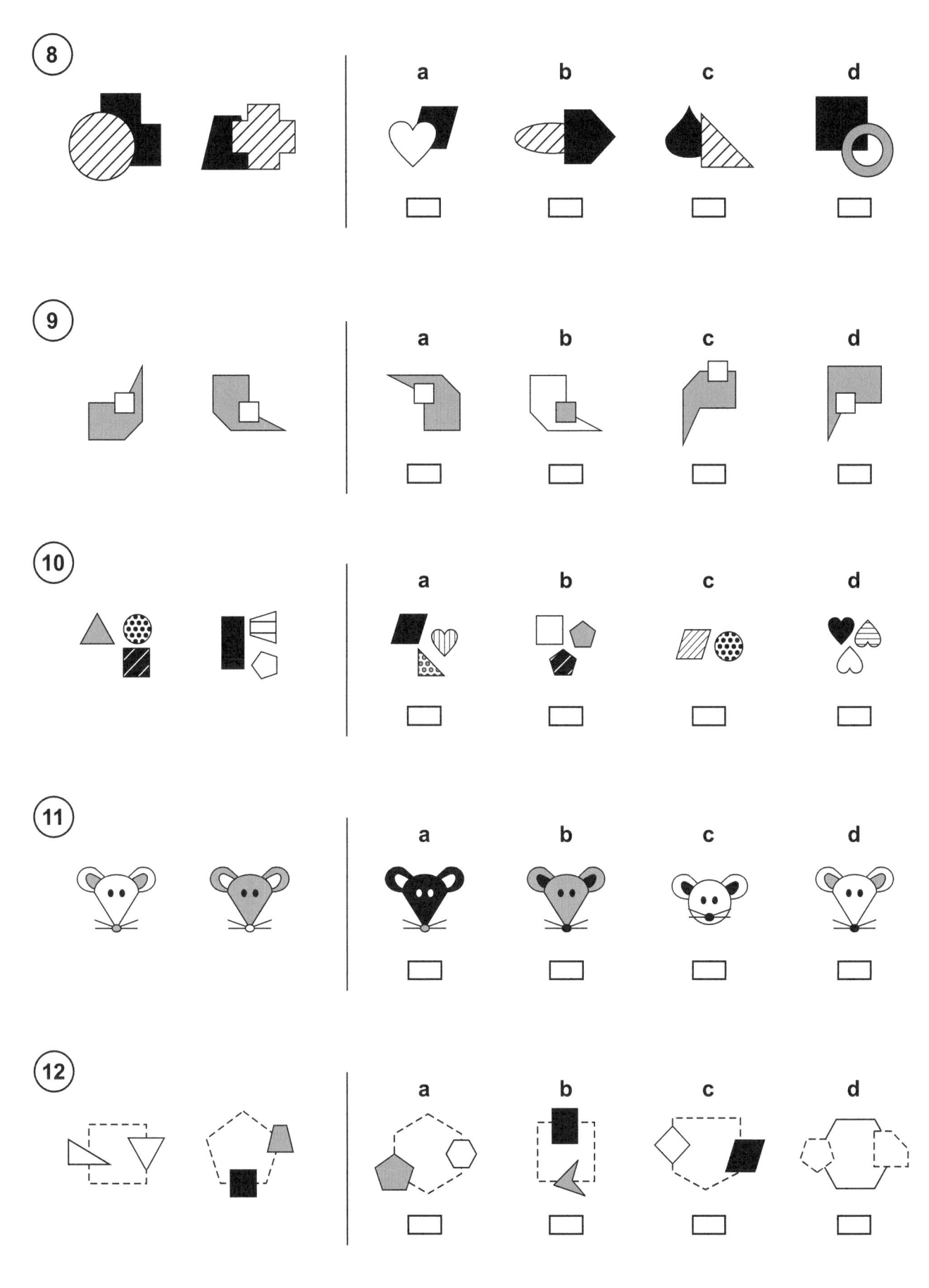

13.

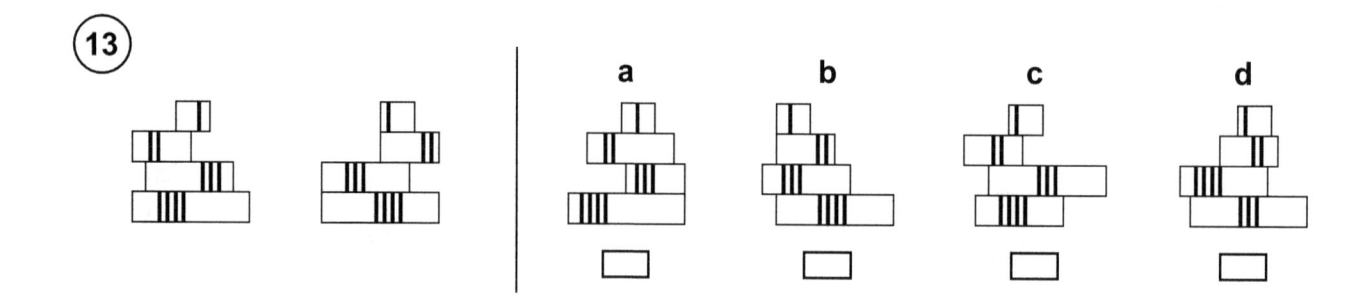

Work out which of the four squares on the right best fits in place of the missing square in the grid:

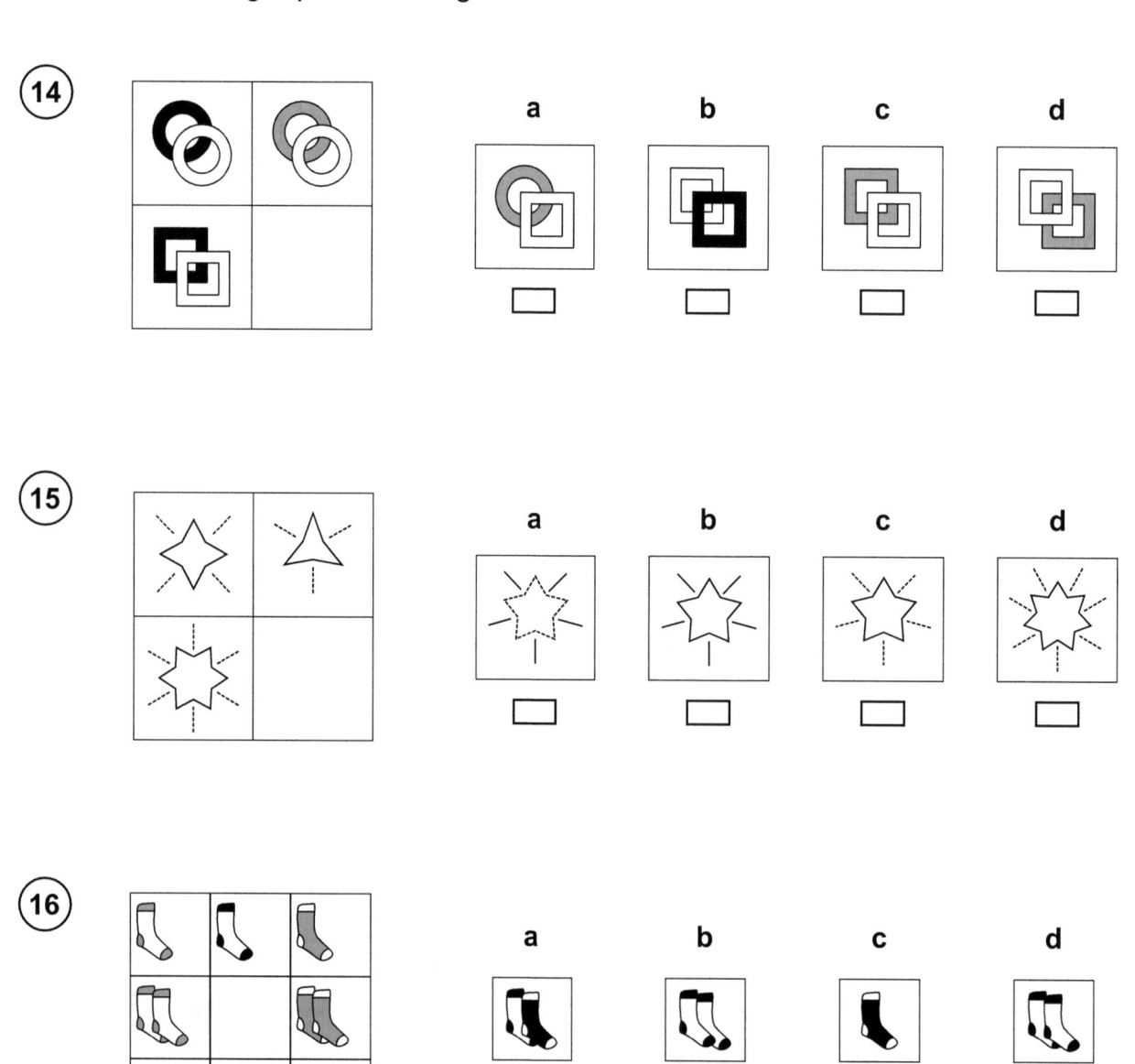

14.

15.

16.

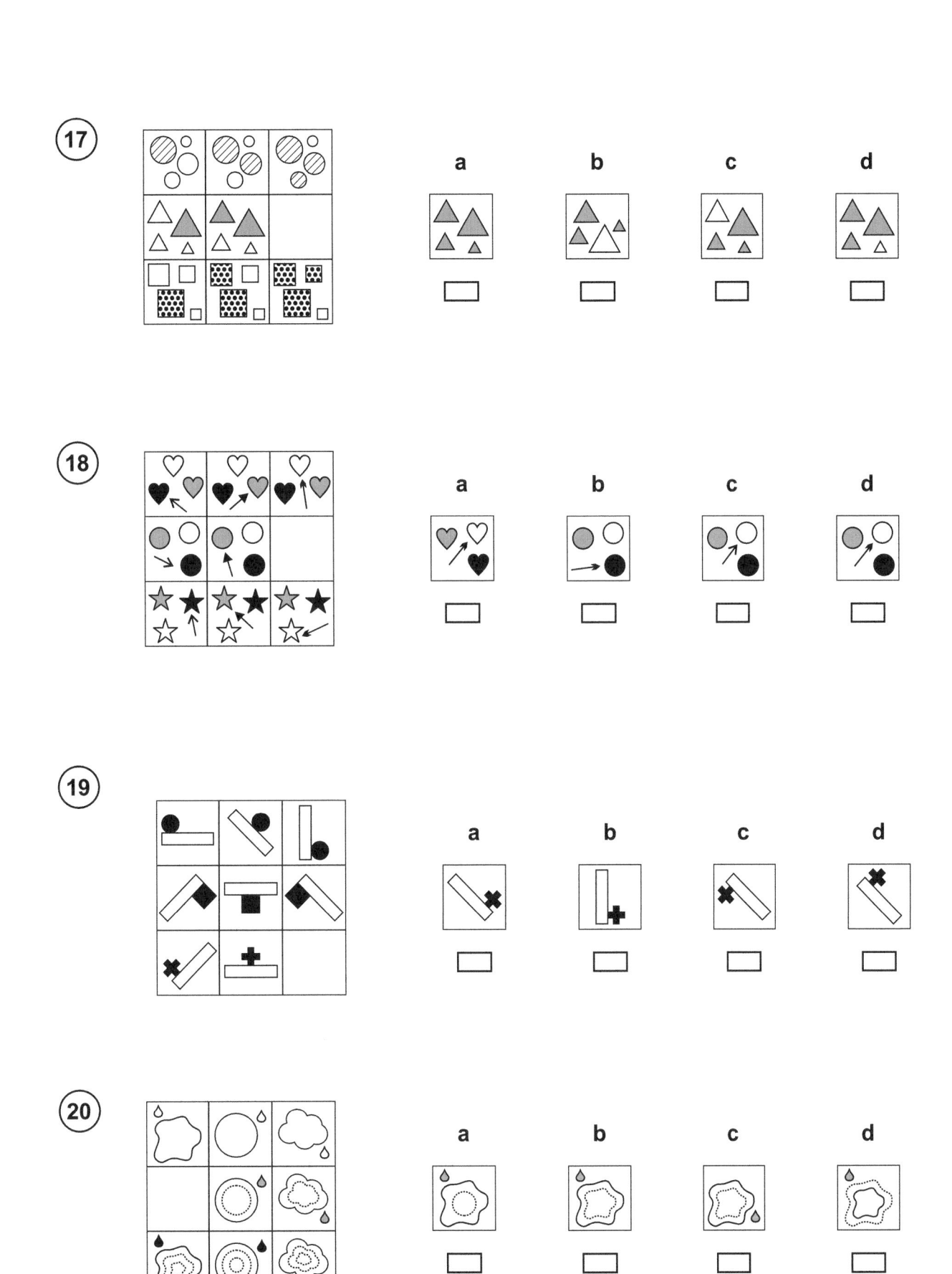

17.

18.

19.

20.

Work out which option would look like the figure on the left if it was rotated:

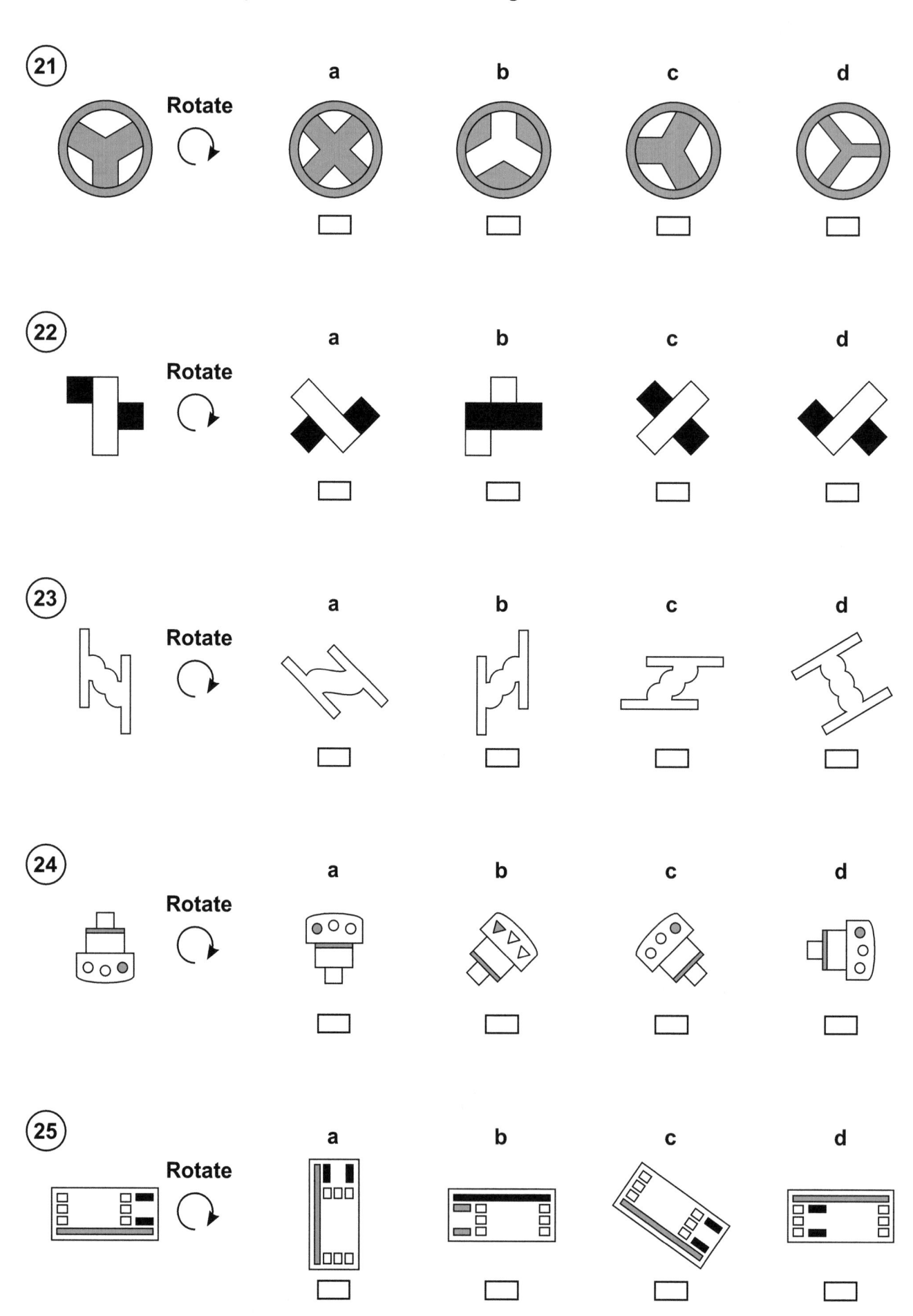

26 Rotate

a   b   c   d

27 Rotate

a   b   c   d

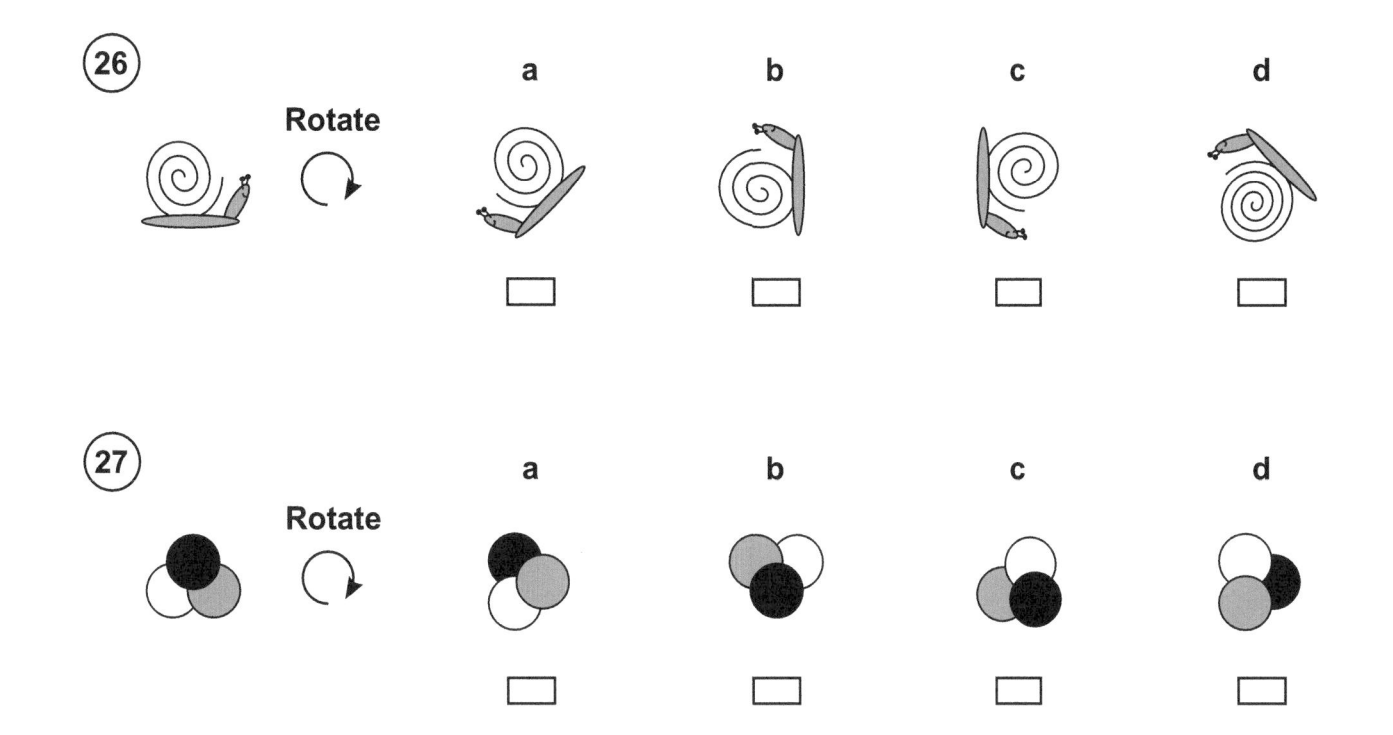

Find the figure in each row that is most unlike the other figures:

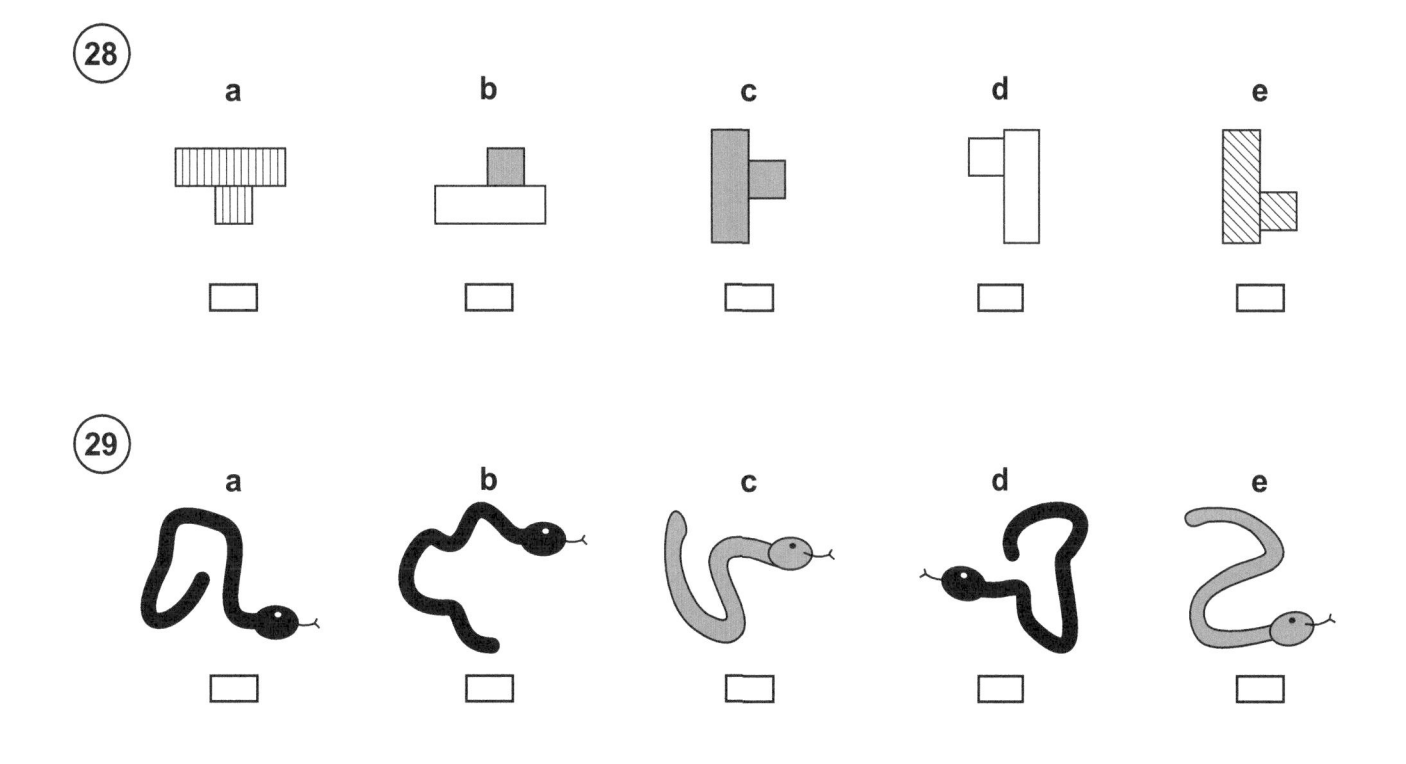

28 a   b   c   d   e

29 a   b   c   d   e

Go to the next question

30) a b c d e

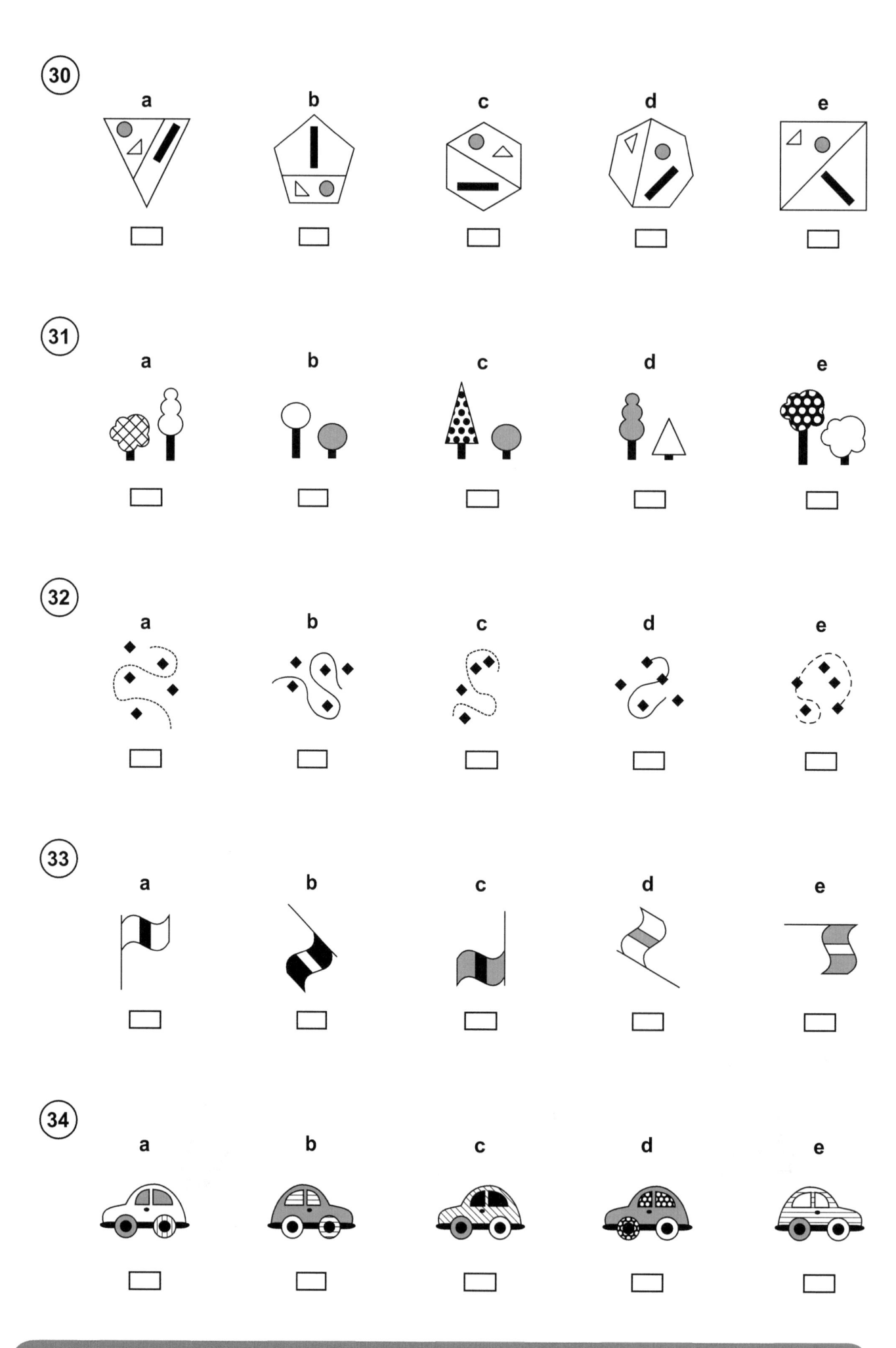

31) a b c d e

32) a b c d e

33) a b c d e

34) a b c d e

Stop — you may check your answers in this section only

CGP

11+ Practice Paper
For Ages 8-9
Set B: Paper 1
For the CEM Test

Read the following:

Do not open this booklet or start the test until you are told to do so.

1. This test can be taken in either multiple-choice or write-in format.

2. If you are taking it as a multiple-choice test, you should mark your answer to each question in pencil on the separate answer sheet. Mark the correct box quickly and neatly using a horizontal line.

3. If you are taking it as a write-in test, you should write your answer to each question in pencil on the paper. Write your answer carefully in the space provided or, if there is a range of options, mark the correct box quickly and neatly using a horizontal line.

4. If you make a mistake, rub it out and mark your new answer clearly.

5. There are six sections in this test.

6. The time allowed for each section is given at the start of that section. You will have a total of 45 minutes to complete the timed sections of the test.

7. Each section includes examples showing you how to answer the questions. You may refer to these examples at any time as you work through the section.

8. Do as many questions as you can. For some questions you will be given a range of options — if you get stuck on one of these questions, choose the answer that you think is most likely to be correct, then move on to the next question. If you get stuck on a question for which no options are given, leave it and move on to the next question. If you have time at the end of the section, go back and have another go at the questions you could not answer.

9. You should do any rough working on a separate piece of paper.

Work carefully, but go as quickly as you can.

Exam Set ELY4PDE1 © CGP 2019

Section 1: Verbal Reasoning — Comprehension 1

Example — Read these example questions. You may return to these examples at any time as you work through this section.

Wojtek the Warrior Bear

1   People have been introduced to many famous bears in the last century, including Paddington, Winnie-the-Pooh and Yogi Bear. However, one extraordinary bear who is seldom mentioned is Corporal Wojtek, who served in the Polish Army during World War Two. Born in Iran in 1942, Wojtek's mother died when he was just a cub.
5   Wojtek was discovered by an Iranian boy and later adopted by Polish soldiers.
    Wojtek, whose name in Polish roughly translates to 'Happy Warrior', travelled with the soldiers to various locations between Iran and Egypt. They continued to foster the bear, and Wojtek grew considerably in height and weight. Despite his size, Wojtek had a very gentle nature. He adored play-wrestling with the soldiers and
10 learnt to salute when greeted. The soldiers found Wojtek to be a welcome distraction from the war.

A According to the passage, which statement about Wojtek is true?

- ☐ A   He was born in Poland.
- ☐ B   He was discovered by Egyptian soldiers.
- ■ C   His mother died when he was young.
- ☐ D   He served in World War One.

B Why do you think the soldiers let Wojtek travel with them?

- ☐ A   They had extra food that needed eating.
- ■ B   He helped take their mind off the conflict.
- ☐ C   They wanted to improve their strength by wrestling him.
- ☐ D   They needed an extra soldier.

End of example questions

⚠ **Wait until you are told to go on** ⚠

You have 12 minutes to complete this section

There are 15 questions in this section

Read the passage carefully and then answer the questions that follow.

The Dragon Kite

1   Sarah liked nothing more than to sit at her bedroom window and watch the world go by on the busy high street outside. From her flat high above the shops, she could watch as all sorts of people hurried by. From babies in prams being pushed by doting parents, to impatient business people on their way to work, nobody
5   escaped her watchful eyes. Her favourite game was to invent stories about the people she saw on the street below. In Sarah's mind, an old woman hobbling past with a huge bag slung over her shoulder became a clever witch, returning home with some secret ingredients for her magic potion. A curious man wearing a long coat and a hat became a master criminal plotting to rob the bank at the end of
10 the road. Ordinary people were transformed in Sarah's mind into a whole host of different characters: a time traveller from the future, a lost princess from a far-off land or an undercover police officer following a suspect. Sarah could sit for hours dreaming of endless possibilities.
    The only thing that could distract Sarah from the adventures in her own
15 imagination were the items that glinted from behind the glass in the toy shop across the road. It was one of those magnificent old-fashioned shops with crumbling gold letters and a fabulous display in the window. When you entered this shop, it was like stepping back in time. Displayed on the mahogany shelves were all sorts of strange and wonderful things, like a skateboard with six wheels, or hand-carved
20 models of dinosaurs. But these treasures paled in comparison to the green kite that stood proudly in the shop's window display. Shaped like a dragon breathing fire, the enormous kite was so life-like that Sarah could imagine climbing aboard the dragon's wings and soaring with the wind up into the sky.
    Sarah didn't tell anybody about the kite, but she would gaze longingly at it
25 whenever she walked past the toy shop window. As soon as she first saw it in the window display, she started saving up her pocket money to buy it. She volunteered for extra chores and gave up buying sweets so that she could save as much money as possible. As her birthday approached, she realised that she would soon have enough money. Her grandma sent her £5 every year as a present, and when
30 that arrived, she would be able to buy it! Knowing this, the wait until her birthday

Passage continues over the page ➡

seemed impossible. She spent hours sitting on the edge of her bed, impatiently counting down the days on her calendar and anxiously running to the window every few minutes to check that the kite was still there.

    One Saturday, just a week before her birthday, Sarah was staring out of her
35 bedroom window at the people below. It was a miserable, rainy, dark day.
"It would be no use having that kite on a day like today," Sarah thought to herself.
As she concentrated again on the street below, she suddenly saw someone crossing the road to go into the toy shop. She couldn't see much of the person because they were hiding beneath an enormous umbrella. They hurried into the shop, jumping to
40 avoid the puddles forming on the pavement as they went. Sarah watched as the toy shop door closed behind the mysterious person.

    Immediately, her imagination got to work. "Perhaps it's a spy on a secret mission. Or a toy maker bringing some new, exciting toys. Maybe they're buying a special present for someone. As long as it's not the kite they're buying," Sarah thought.
45 "They can buy anything else — just not the kite!"

    Struggling to see through the heavy rain, she watched as the person pointed to something in the window. To her horror, the owner of the toy shop reached over and took the kite from its place in the display. Moments later, the strange person stepped outside with the kite carefully wrapped in a bag under their arm. Sarah's heart was
50 pounding. All of a sudden, a gust of wind caught the person's umbrella and Sarah was able to see the face that had been hidden underneath it. She recognised the person at once. It was her dad! Struggling to control his umbrella in the wind, her dad glanced around him and caught sight of Sarah watching him from the window. Quickly realising that she'd seen everything, he smiled and put his finger to his lips.
55 A grin spread across her face. It looked like she was going to get the kite for her birthday after all.

Answer these questions about the text. You can refer back to the text if you need to.
Pick the best answer and draw a line through the rectangle next to it.

(1) What does the narrator mean when they say that Sarah liked to "watch the world go by" (lines 1-2)?

- [ ] A Sarah liked looking at the sky.
- [ ] B Sarah liked to watch people going about their daily business.
- [ ] C Sarah liked to waste time staring blankly out of the window.
- [ ] D Sarah liked to look at the shops on her road.

(2) According to the text, which of the following statements must be true?

- [ ] A The old woman Sarah saw was a witch.
- [ ] B Someone robbed the bank on Sarah's road.
- [ ] C Sarah lived on a busy street.
- [ ] D Sarah lived next door to a toy shop.

(3) What was special about the toy shop near Sarah's flat?

- [ ] A It sold special video games.
- [ ] B It was full of unusual toys.
- [ ] C It was dark and mysterious.
- [ ] D It was the biggest toy shop in the town.

(4) "these treasures paled in comparison to the green kite" (line 20). This means that:

- [ ] A Sarah thought the kite was better than the other toys in the shop.
- [ ] B the kite was more expensive than the other toys in the shop.
- [ ] C the kite was bigger than the other toys in the shop.
- [ ] D Sarah couldn't see any of the toys except for the kite.

(5) Which word best describes the kite?

- [ ] A Painted
- [ ] B Gold
- [ ] C Large
- [ ] D Old

Go to the next question ⇨

6 Why did Sarah do extra chores?

- [ ] **A** Because she had been naughty
- [ ] **B** Because she wanted to please her parents
- [ ] **C** Because she wanted to get extra sweets
- [ ] **D** Because she wanted to earn extra pocket money

7 Which of the following is not mentioned in the text?

- [ ] **A** The number of wheels on the skateboard in the toy shop
- [ ] **B** The shape of the kite Sarah wanted to buy
- [ ] **C** The amount of money Sarah's grandma gave her every year
- [ ] **D** The date of Sarah's birthday

8 Sarah spent hours "counting down the days on her calendar" (line 32).
This suggests that:

- [ ] **A** Sarah wasn't very good at counting.
- [ ] **B** Sarah wished that time wasn't passing so quickly.
- [ ] **C** Sarah couldn't wait for her birthday to come.
- [ ] **D** Sarah was trying to stop herself from looking out of the window.

9 According to the text, which of the following statements is true?

- [ ] **A** The mysterious person went into the toy shop to steal the kite.
- [ ] **B** The toy shop was closed when the mysterious person arrived.
- [ ] **C** It was raining when the mysterious person went into the toy shop.
- [ ] **D** Sarah followed the mysterious person into the toy shop.

10 How was Sarah able to recognise her dad?

- [ ] **A** He took off his hat.
- [ ] **B** His umbrella was blown aside by the wind.
- [ ] **C** Sarah recognised his coat.
- [ ] **D** He waved to her when he came out of the shop.

11 Why do you think Sarah's dad "put his finger to his lips" (line 54)?

- A Sarah was being too noisy.
- B He had to wipe rain off his face.
- C The kite was supposed to be a birthday surprise.
- D He was thinking about what to do next.

12 Which word best describes how Sarah was feeling at the end of the passage?

- A Frustrated
- B Puzzled
- C Indifferent
- D Relieved

13 What does "watchful" mean (line 5)?

- A Shining
- B Attentive
- C Suspicious
- D Fearful

14 What does "glinted" mean (line 15)?

- A Twinkled
- B Fluttered
- C Smiled
- D Revolved

15 Sarah gazed at the kite "longingly" (line 24). This means that:

- A She was bored of looking at the kite.
- B She couldn't see the kite well from her bedroom window.
- C She wished that she had the kite.
- D She kept seeing the kite everywhere she went.

Stop — you may check your answers in this section only

Section 2: Verbal Reasoning — Comprehension 2

You have 8 minutes to complete this section

There are 10 questions in this section

Read the passage carefully and then answer the questions that follow.

Niagara Falls

1   At the border between the United States and Canada sit three enormous waterfalls, known collectively as Niagara Falls. Two of them are located in the US, while the biggest waterfall — the Horseshoe Falls — crosses the border, but is mostly in Canada. At the highest point, the water from the top drops over 50 metres into the river below. However,
5   the waterfalls in Niagara are far from the world's tallest. At an awe-inspiring 979 metres tall, Angel Falls in Venezuela is widely accepted as the world's tallest waterfall.

      What makes Niagara Falls special is the enormous amount of water that crashes down from the waterfalls — around 3000 tonnes a second. The water that comes surging along the river doesn't just look impressive. Since the 1800s, the flow of water
10   has also been used to generate electricity. Some of the water is channelled away from the waterfalls and used to turn large turbines, which produce vast amounts of energy.

      Many people have attempted to brave the strong currents and travel over the Falls from the top to the bottom far below. This is extremely dangerous and has often led to deadly results. The first person to survive the drop was 63-year-old school teacher
15   Annie Edson Taylor, who went over the Falls in a barrel on her birthday in 1901. Astonishingly, Annie climbed out of the barrel without serious injuries, although she was very bruised and frightened.

      Taylor is not the only thrill-seeker to choose Niagara Falls for their death-defying stunts. In 1859, thousands of people came to watch as a famous French tightrope
20   walker known as Charles Blondin walked on a tightrope across the Niagara Gorge. Blondin was so certain of his ability as a tightrope walker that he went on to make many more crossings and performed a whole range of unbelievable stunts in the process. These included walking backwards on the tightrope, as well as crossing the tightrope while blindfolded, while pushing a wheelbarrow and while wearing stilts.

25   Although Blondin's performances attracted large crowds, the Falls don't need daredevils like him to help them draw in tourists. Millions of people visit Niagara Falls each year to admire the amazing views or to take a boat trip to see the waterfalls close up. One well-known boat tour is called the 'Maid of the Mist', and its success is unsurprising — with the breathtaking beauty and incredible power of the waterfalls, it's
30   no wonder that Niagara Falls is such a popular attraction.

Answer these questions about the text. You can refer back to the text if you need to. Pick the best answer and draw a line through the rectangle next to it.

1 Which of the following best describes Niagara Falls?

- A The tallest waterfall in the world
- B A collection of three waterfalls
- C A group of hundreds of small waterfalls
- D A large waterfall in the United States

2 According to the text, which country do most people agree is home to the world's tallest waterfall?

- A France
- B The United States
- C Venezuela
- D Canada

3 In what year did Annie Edson Taylor travel over the Falls?

- A 1800
- B 1846
- C 1859
- D 1901

4 According to the text, which of the following statements is false?

- A Annie Edson Taylor was a teacher.
- B Annie Edson Taylor went over Niagara Falls on her birthday.
- C Annie Edson Taylor was not seriously hurt by her trip over the Falls.
- D Annie Edson Taylor went over Niagara Falls in a special boat.

5 Which word best describes how Annie Edson Taylor felt after she travelled over the Falls?

- A Calm
- B Shaken
- C Excited
- D Overjoyed

Go to the next question

6 According to the text, which of the following stunts did Charles Blondin successfully perform?

- ☐ A Tightrope walking across the Niagara Gorge on his hands
- ☐ B Falling from the top of the waterfall in a barrel
- ☐ C Tightrope walking across the Niagara Gorge on stilts
- ☐ D Swimming from the Canadian side of the Falls to the US side

7 What do lines 25-28 tell you about the tourists who visit Niagara today?

- ☐ A They come to look at the beautiful scenery.
- ☐ B They come to watch Charles Blondin perform.
- ☐ C They visit in order to try crazy stunts.
- ☐ D They visit Niagara Falls to go swimming in the river.

8 According to the text, what is the Maid of the Mist?

- ☐ A The name of one of the waterfalls
- ☐ B The name of a statue above the Falls
- ☐ C The name of a boat tour that takes you to see the waterfalls
- ☐ D The nickname given to Annie Edson Taylor after she went over the top of the Falls

9 What does the word "surging" mean (line 9)?

- ☐ A Spinning
- ☐ B Trickling
- ☐ C Freezing
- ☐ D Rushing

10 What does the word "astonishingly" mean (line 16)?

- ☐ A Unfortunately
- ☐ B Surprisingly
- ☐ C Mysteriously
- ☐ D Painfully

Stop — you may check your answers in this section only

BLANK PAGE

Section 3: Verbal Reasoning — Odd One Out

Example Read this example question. You may return to this example at any time as you work through this section.

Three of the words in each list are linked.
Mark the rectangle under the word that is **not** related to these three.

A) sister   brother   family   cousin

⚠️ **Wait until you are told to go on** ⚠️

⏱ **You have 6 minutes to complete this section** ⏱

There are 18 questions in this section

Three of the words in each list are linked.
Mark the rectangle under the word that is **not** related to these three.

1) fast   swift   rapid   sharp

2) spanner   hammered   saw   drill

3) ankle   toe   heel   nose

4) supermarket   baker   butcher   grocer

5) English   Multiplication   History   Geography

6) Spain   London   China   Russia

7) chalk   water   paint   crayon

8) seesaw slide go-kart swings
☐   ☐   ☐   ☐

9) arm wing tail horn
☐   ☐   ☐   ☐

10) run hike cycle sprint
☐   ☐   ☐   ☐

11) America Atlantic Pacific Indian
☐   ☐   ☐   ☐

12) atlas textbook dictionary poster
☐   ☐   ☐   ☐

13) doormat painting mirror photograph
☐   ☐   ☐   ☐

14) buddy neighbour pal chum
☐   ☐   ☐   ☐

15) saucepan kettle toaster microwave
☐   ☐   ☐   ☐

16) amusing entertainment funny humorous
☐   ☐   ☐   ☐

17) bake fry chop grill
☐   ☐   ☐   ☐

18) outstanding bizarre weird odd
☐   ☐   ☐   ☐

Stop — you may check your answers in this section only

Section 4: Verbal Reasoning — Shuffled Sentences

Example Read this example question. You may return to this example at any time as you work through this section.

Rearrange the words so that each sentence makes sense.
Mark the rectangle under the word which does **not** fit into the sentence.

A it   for   time   was   late   bed
 ☐   ☐   ☐   ☐   ■   ☐

The remaining words can be rearranged to make the sentence: 'It was time for bed.'

⚠ Wait until you are told to go on ⚠

You have 6 minutes to complete this section

There are 15 questions in this section

Rearrange the words so that each sentence makes sense.
Mark the rectangle under the word which does **not** fit into the sentence.

1 she   down   waiting   the   long   sprinted   path

2 remember   actor   performed   couldn't   the   lines   his

3 mansion   is   by   haunted   ghosts   the   terrify

4 not   poisonous   snakes   threat   all   are

5 to   Satoshi   cards   played   trading   loved   collect

6 on   hated   Joel   pizza   like   mushrooms   his

7) are sugary for taste your bad sweets teeth

8) stuck the was on finish Millie puzzle final

9) he tyre car very the drove slowly

10) looked the very fought similar brothers

11) hole in stripes has it sock my a

12) people speaking made public her nervous

13) over is best tonight my friend sleeping bed

14) told jokes hilarious many at dinner cackle Zara

15) started family his Nathan visited miss to

Stop — you may check your answers in this section only

Section 5: Verbal Reasoning — Cloze

Example Read these example questions. You may return to these examples at any time as you work through this section.

Tea is often thought of as a traditional English drink. (A) ☐ Despite
■ However , it was
☐ Also

popular in China centuries before it (B) ☐ drunk
☐ travelled in Europe.
■ arrived

⚠ Wait until you are told to go on ⚠

⏱ You have 6 minutes to complete this section ⏱

There are 18 questions in this section

Have you ever (1) ☐ been
☐ heard the expression "dead as a dodo"? It refers to the
☐ see

flightless bird, the dodo, which (2) ☐ has
☐ have been extinct for (3) ☐ over
☐ ages
☐ were
☐ between

300 years. This (4) ☐ tells
☐ show that there aren't any dodos still alive in the world
☐ means

today. Dodos were large birds with small wings and long, curved beaks. They

(5) ☐ stay
☐ home on the island of Mauritius off the east (6) ☐ coast
☐ mountain of Africa.
☐ lived
☐ forest

Until humans (7) ☐ sailed / ☐ arrived / ☐ left   on Mauritius in the 1500s, dodos were

(8) ☐ able / ☐ possible / ☐ hard   to survive with no natural predators to trouble them.

However, when explorers from Europe came to Mauritius, things started to

(9) ☐ change / ☐ developing / ☐ increase . (10) ☐ Although / ☐ Despite / ☐ But   people did hunt some of the dodos

for food, it is (11) ☐ believed / ☐ really / ☐ unsure   that the biggest (12) ☐ damaging / ☐ threat / ☐ prey   to dodos

came from the animals that people had (13) ☐ bring / ☐ brought / ☐ take   with them to the

island. These animals, (14) ☐ including / ☐ for / ☐ such   pigs and rats, ate the dodos' eggs and

stole a (15) ☐ all / ☐ piece / ☐ lot   of their food. By the middle of the 1600s, there weren't

(16) ☐ several / ☐ many / ☐ none   dodos left (17) ☐ dead / ☐ alive / ☐ free . Nobody knows (18) ☐ exactly / ☐ generally / ☐ probably

when the last dodo died, but the last recorded sighting of one was in 1662.

Stop — you may check your answers in this section only

Section 6: Non-Verbal Reasoning

Example Read these example questions. You may return to these examples at any time as you work through this section.

A) Work out which option is the 3D figure viewed from the right.

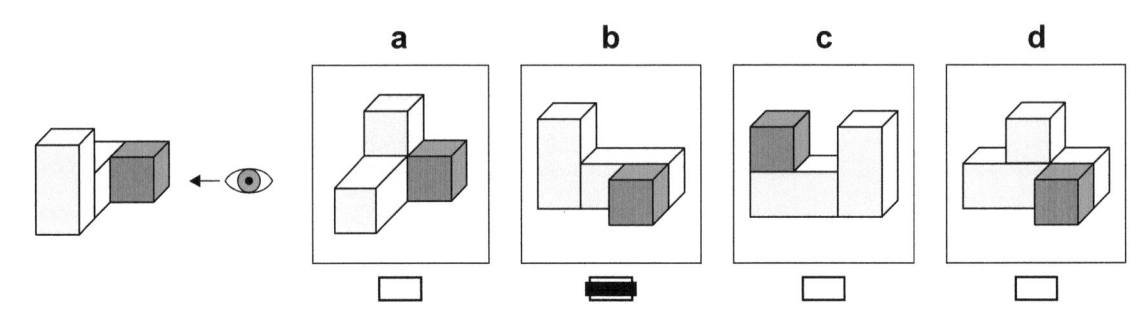

B) Work out which option shows the figure on the left when folded along the dotted line.

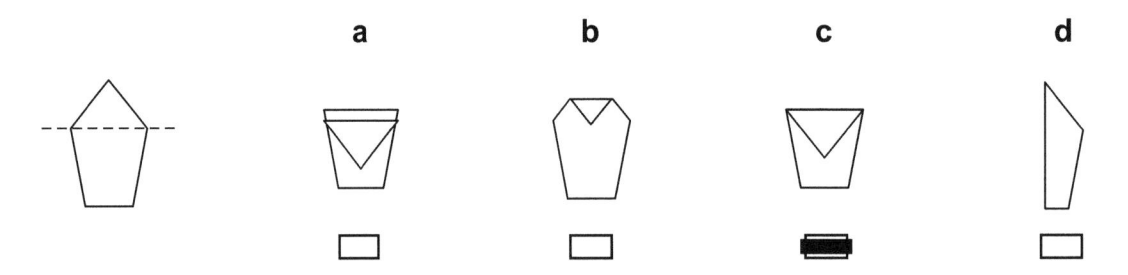

C) Work out which option is a top-down 2D view of the 3D figure on the left.

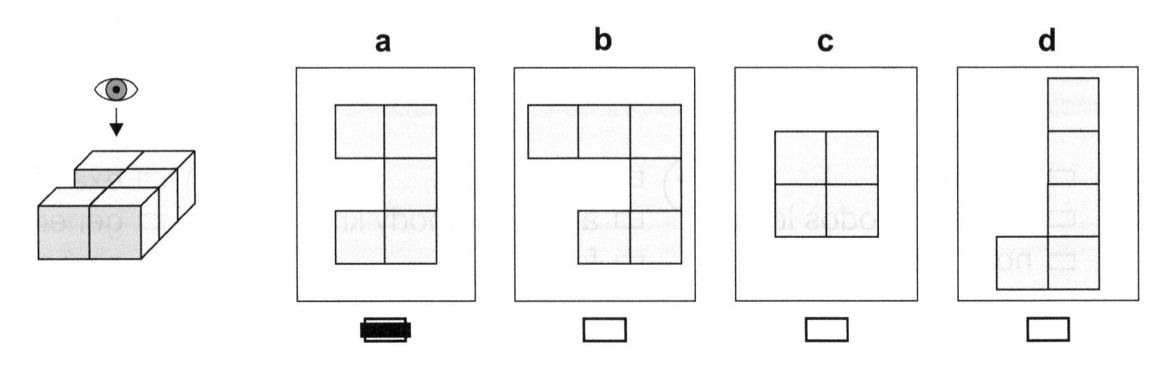

Wait until you are told to go on

You have 7 minutes to complete this section

There are 19 questions in this section

Work out which option is the 3D figure viewed from the right.

1.   a 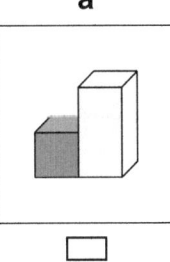   b 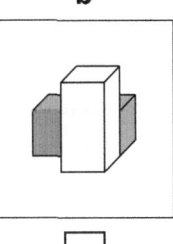   c 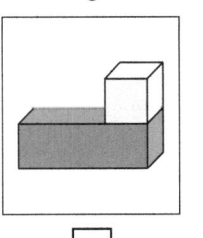   d

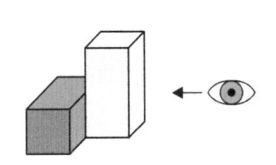

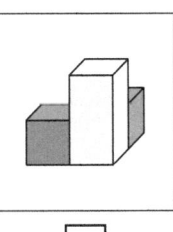

2. 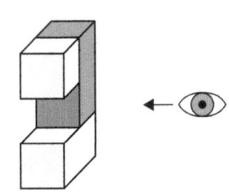   a 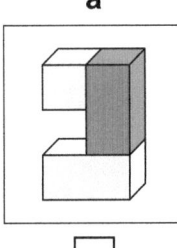   b 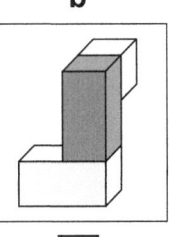   c 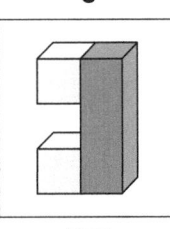   d

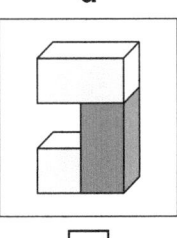

3. 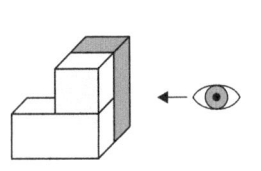   a 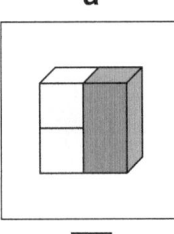   b 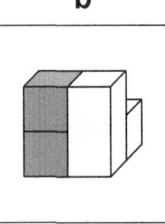   c 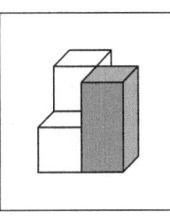   d

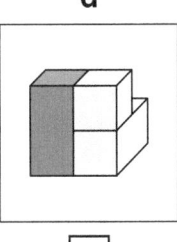

4. 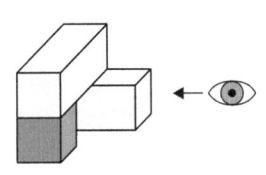   a 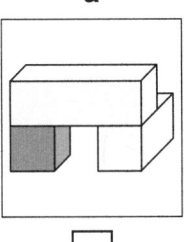   b 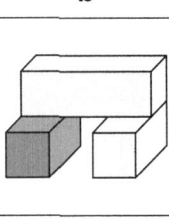   c 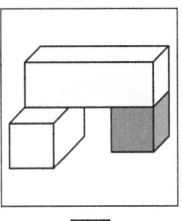   d

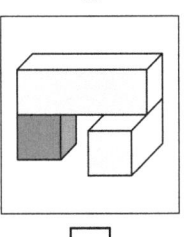

Go to the next question

(5) a b c d

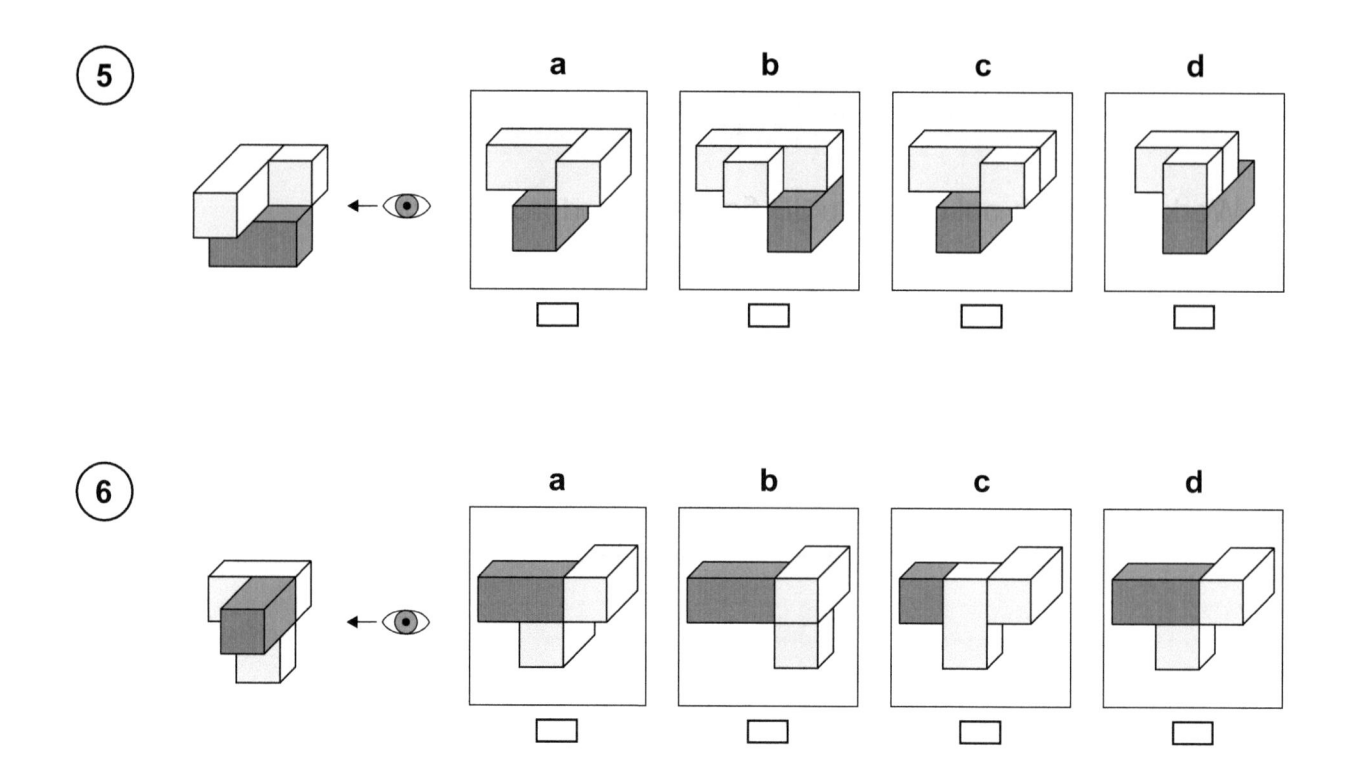

(6) a b c d

Work out which option shows the figure on the left when folded along the dotted line.

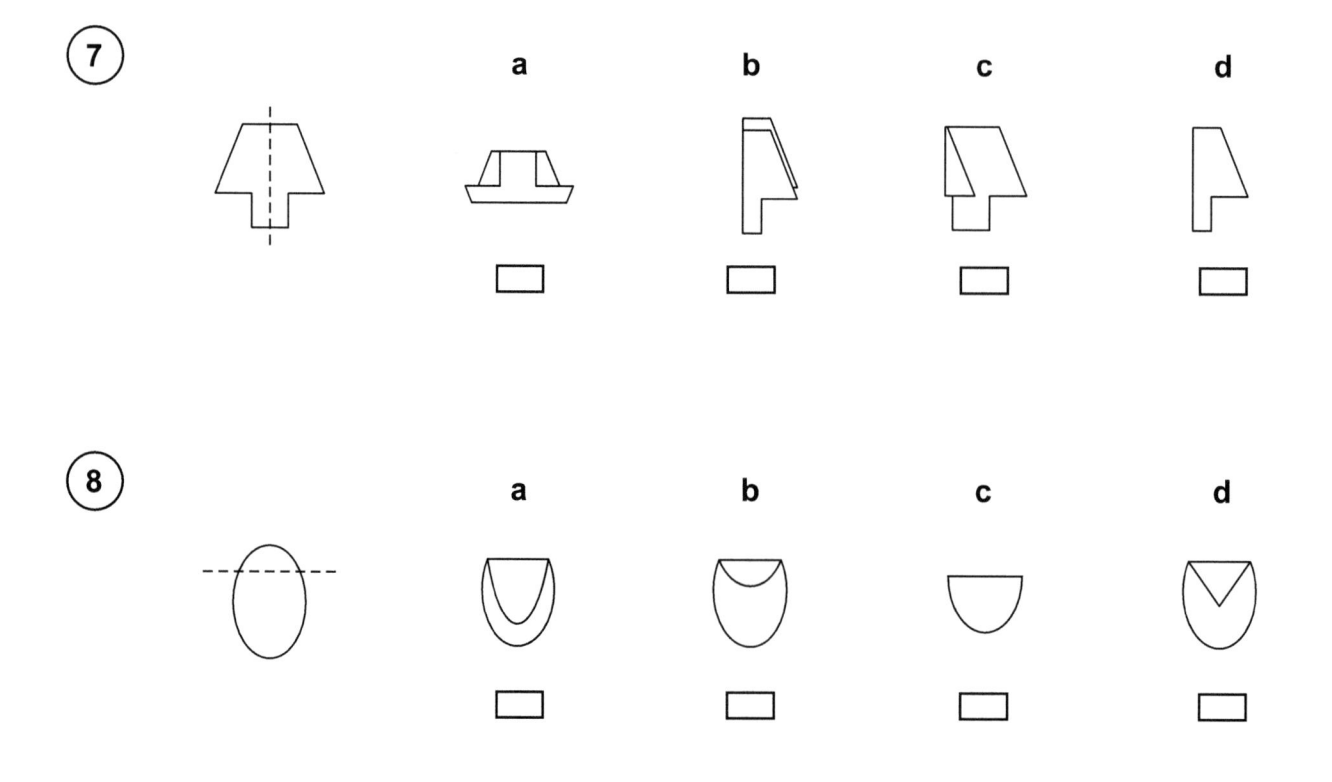

(7) a b c d

(8) a b c d

(9) a b c d

(10) a b c d

(11) a b c d

(12) a b c d

Go to the next question ➡

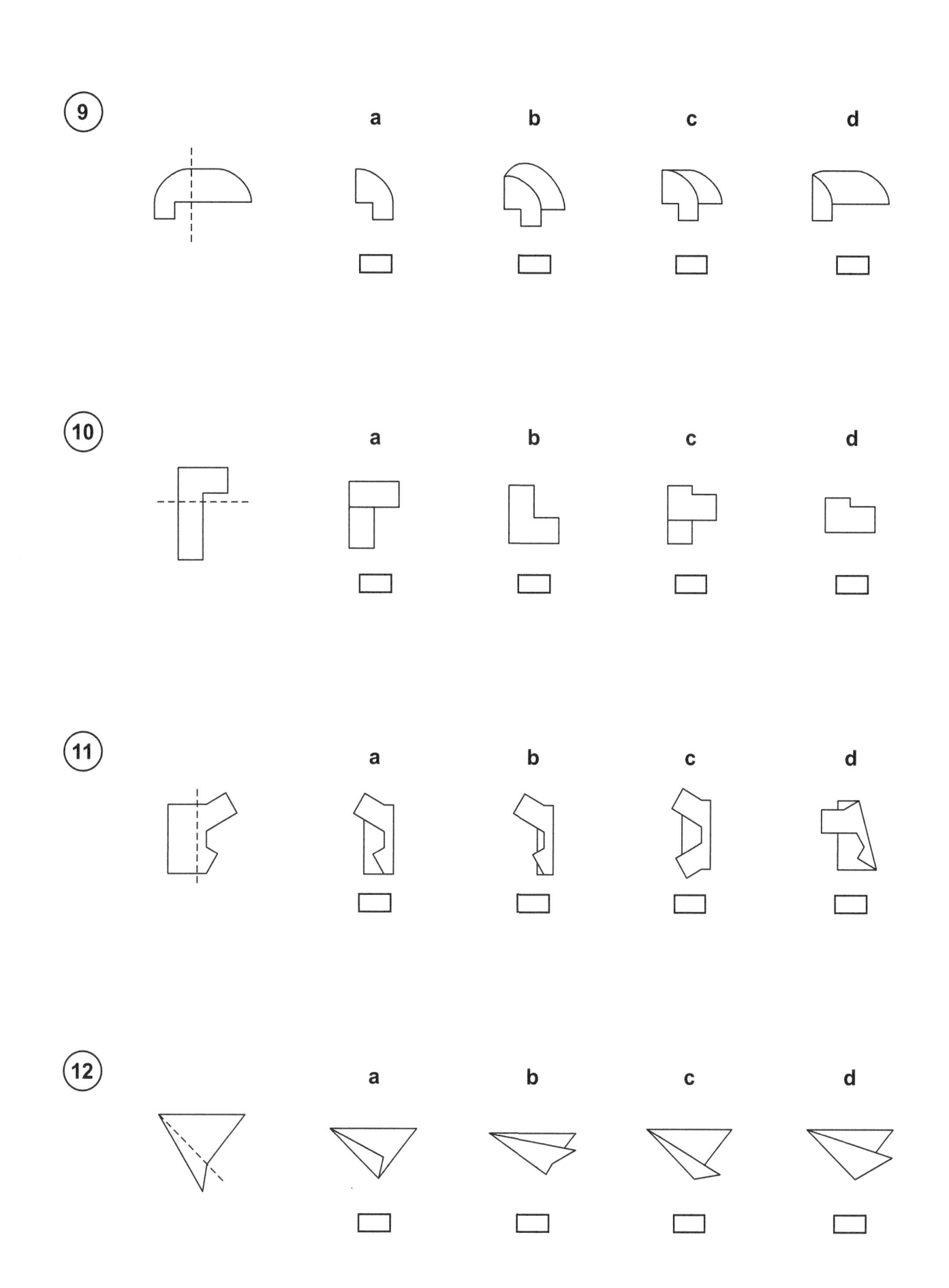

13 a b c d

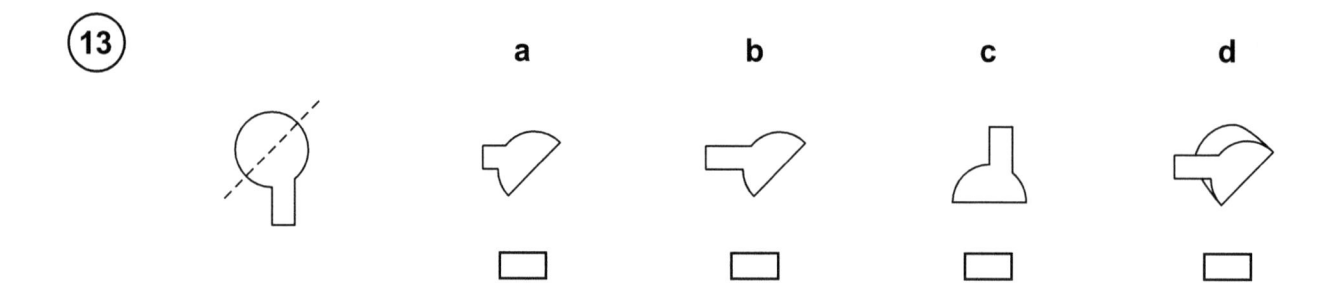

Work out which option is a top-down 2D view of the 3D figure on the left.

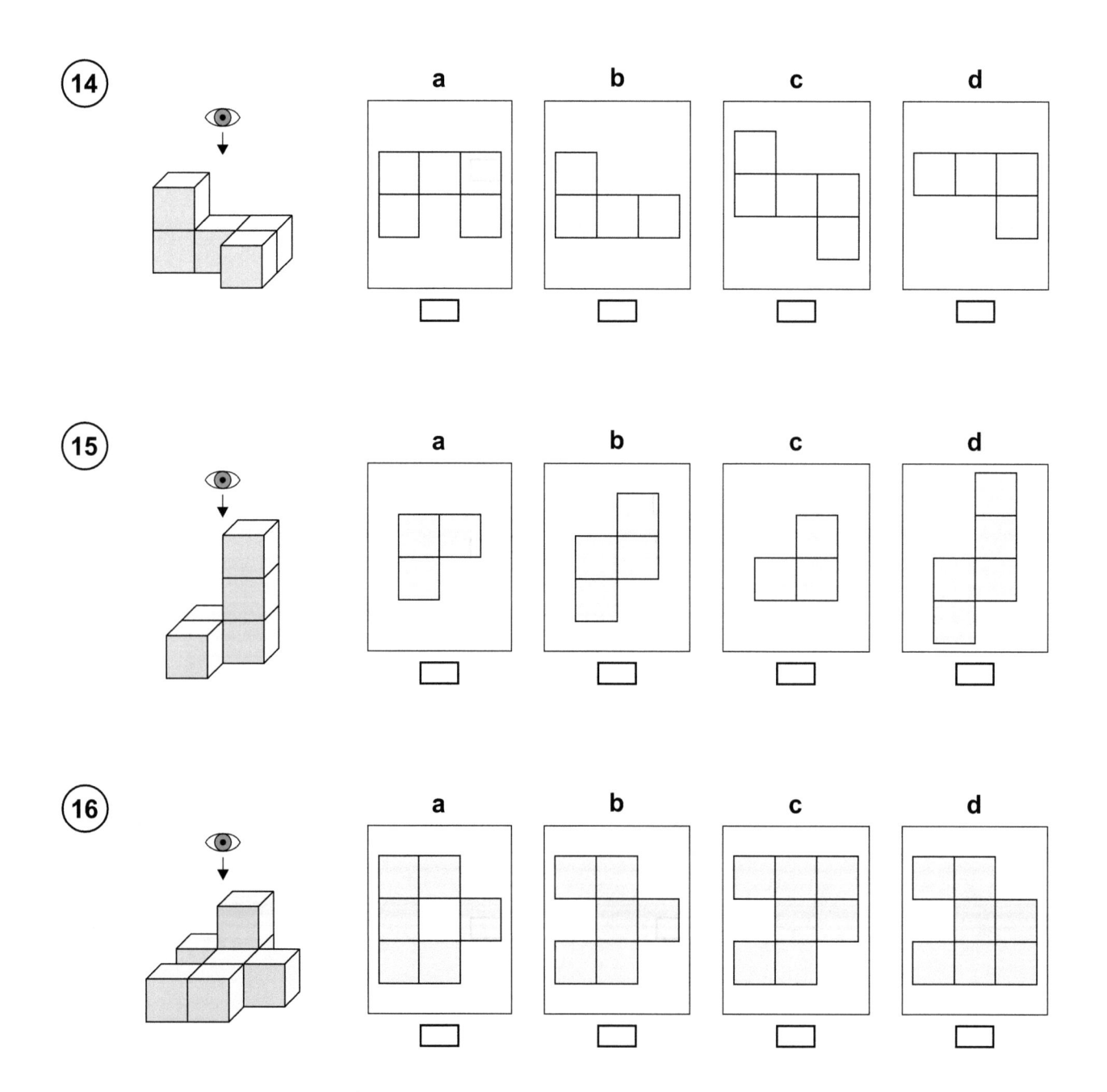

14 a b c d

15 a b c d

16 a b c d

11+ / CEM / 8-9 / B / Paper 1   22   © CGP 2019

17 a b c d

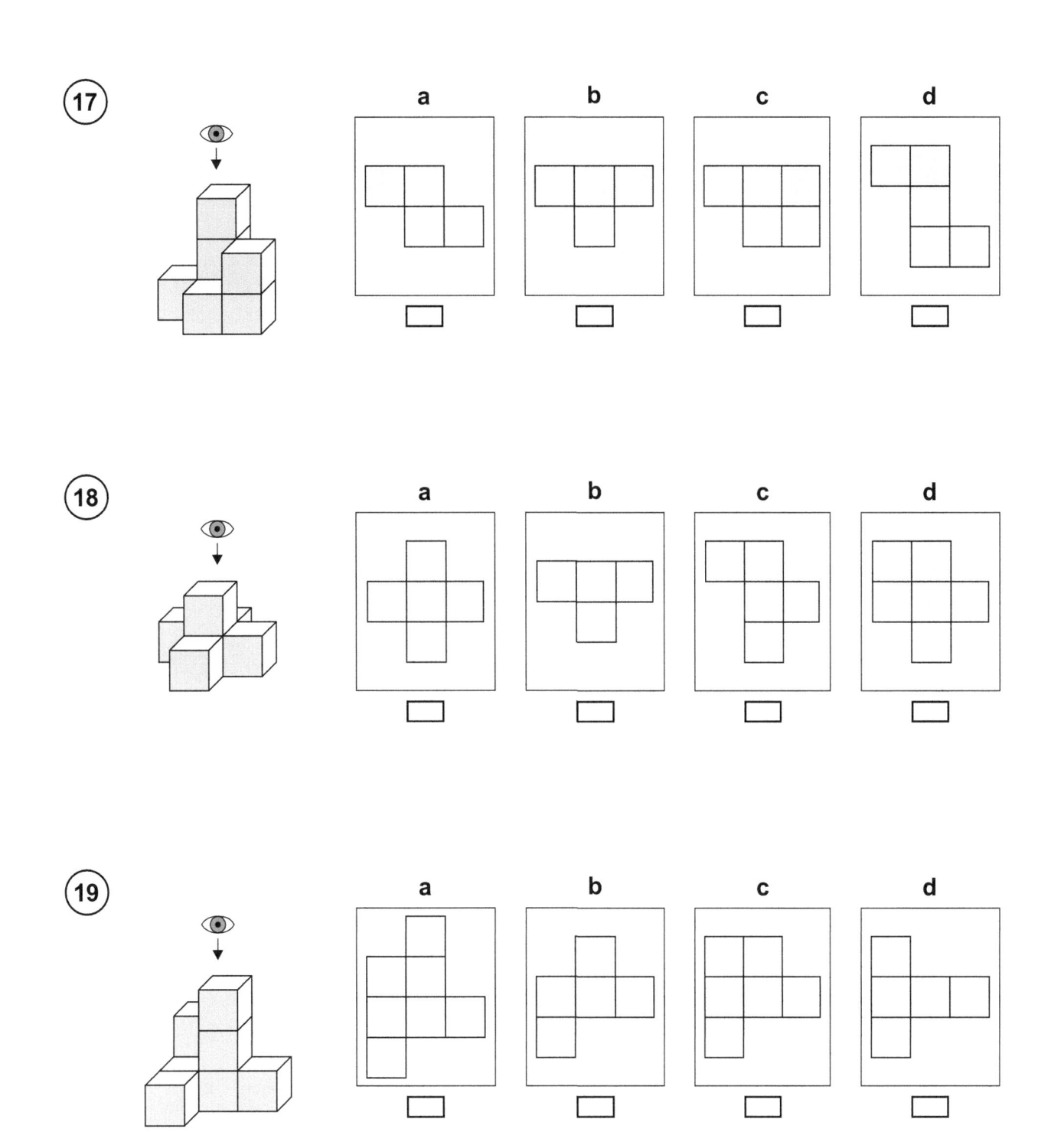

18 a b c d

19 a b c d

Stop — you may check your answers in this section only

BLANK PAGE

CGP

11+ Practice Paper
For Ages 8-9
Set B: Paper 2
For the CEM Test

Read the following:

Do not open this booklet or start the test until you are told to do so.

1. This test can be taken in either multiple-choice or write-in format.

2. If you are taking it as a multiple-choice test, you should mark your answer to each question in pencil on the separate answer sheet. Mark the correct box quickly and neatly using a horizontal line.

3. If you are taking it as a write-in test, you should write your answer to each question in pencil on the paper. Write your answer carefully in the space provided or, if there is a range of options, mark the correct box quickly and neatly using a horizontal line.

4. If you make a mistake, rub it out and mark your new answer clearly.

5. There are three sections in this test.

6. The time allowed for each section is given at the start of that section. You will have a total of 45 minutes to complete the timed sections of the test.

7. Each section includes examples showing you how to answer the questions. You may refer to these examples at any time as you work through the section.

8. Do as many questions as you can. For some questions you will be given a range of options — if you get stuck on one of these questions, choose the answer that you think is most likely to be correct, then move on to the next question. If you get stuck on a question for which no options are given, leave it and move on to the next question. If you have time at the end of the section, go back and have another go at the questions you could not answer.

9. You should do any rough working on a separate piece of paper.

Work carefully, but go as quickly as you can.

Exam Set ELY4PDE1 © CGP 2019

Section 1: Verbal Reasoning — Antonyms

Example Read this example question. You may return to this example at any time as you work through this section.

Choose the word which means the opposite, or nearly the opposite, of the word on the left.

A) hot   angry   cough   **cold**   shiver

⚠️ **Wait until you are told to go on** ⚠️

⏱️ **You have 5 minutes to complete this section** ⏱️

There are 15 questions in this section

Choose the word which means the opposite, or nearly the opposite, of the word on the left.

1) hurry   quicker   calm   messy   delay

2) maybe   perhaps   definitely   sometimes   unlikely

3) irritate   soothe   stress   heal   respect

4) crucial   common   unnecessary   awkward   boring

5) drag   pull   shuffle   throw   push

6) wobbly   strong   steady   shaky   flexible

7) **unsure** right certain wise confused

8) **aid** cure dislike harm ruin

9) **child** teenager baby human parent

10) **swell** shrink widen ache recover

11) **hairy** rough furry spotty bald

12) **hire** employ manage work fire

13) **city** town seaside countryside nation

14) **trendy** old cheap second-hand unfashionable

15) **cause** make continue prevent encourage

Stop — you may check your answers in this section only

Section 2: Verbal Reasoning — Synonyms

Example Read this example question. You may return to this example at any time as you work through this section.

Complete the word on the right so that it means the same, or nearly the same, as the word on the left.

(A) mumble w h i s p e r

⚠ **Wait until you are told to go on** ⚠

⏱ **You have 6 minutes to complete this section** ⏱

There are 15 questions in this section

Complete the word on the right so that it means the same, or nearly the same, as the word on the left.

(1) raise   i _ c _ e a _ e

(2) often   r _ g _ l _ r l _

(3) enjoyment   p _ _ _ s u _ e

(4) wrong   _ n _ o r _ _ c t

(5) say   m _ n _ _ o n

(6) image   p _ _ t _ r e

7) edge — b o r d e r

8) burnt — s c o r c h e d

9) show — d i s p l a y

10) prize — a w a r d

11) spot — p i m p l e

12) piece — c h u n k

13) boss — e m p l o y e r

14) perfect — i d e a l

15) fence — b a r r i e r

Section 3: Numerical Reasoning

Example Read these example questions. You may return to these examples at any time as you work through this section.

A Fill in the missing number to make this calculation correct: 8 × [ ][5] = 40

B Which Roman numeral means 64?

LXV ☐   LXVI ☐   XLIV ☐   LXIV ▬   XLVI ☐

C Mandy records how far a snail has moved every two minutes. She makes the graph below with her results.

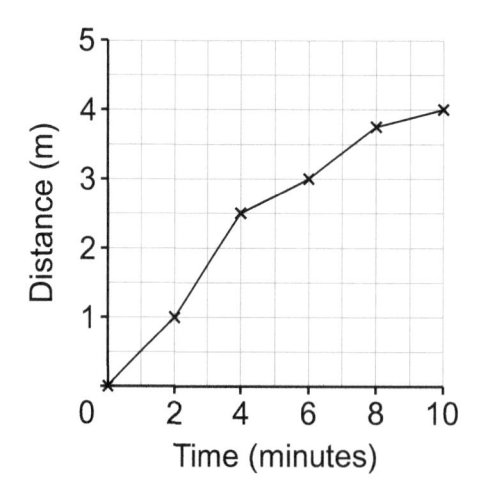

C1 How far did the snail move in the first 6 minutes?

[ ][3] m

C2 In what time period did the snail move the furthest?

0-2 minutes ☐   2-4 minutes ▬   4-6 minutes ☐   6-8 minutes ☐   8-10 minutes ☐

⚠ Wait until you are told to go on ⚠

You have 34 minutes to complete this section

This section contains single-part and multi-part questions.
There are 30 questions in this section

1) The box below shows the greatest depths of four seas.

Name	North Sea	Red Sea	Black Sea	Sea of Japan
Depth (m)	700	3040	2212	3742

Sheila lists the seas in order of their depths, from largest to smallest.
Which is the correct list?

☐ Japan, Black, Red, North

☐ North, Black, Red, Japan

☐ Japan, Red, Black, North

☐ Black, Red, Japan, North

2) The temperature of Peter's oven is controlled by a dial.
The current temperature selected is 140 °C, as shown below.

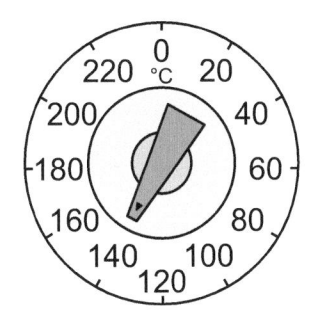

Peter turns the dial one quarter turn anticlockwise.
What is the new temperature that Peter has chosen?

☐☐☐ °C

Go to the next question

③ Hannah says:

"My number has 3 in the thousands column and 8 in the tens column."

Which of these could be Hannah's number?

    3870   31 085   3680   382   38 094

④ Look at this shape.

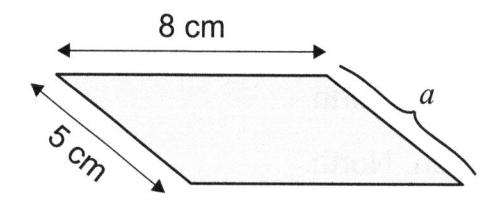

a) What is the name of the shape?

    square   rhombus   parallelogram   kite   rectangle

b) What is the length of the side labelled a?

☐☐ cm

⑤ Which whole number has been circled on this number line?

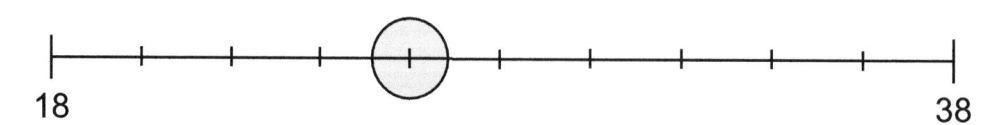

☐☐

6) Some children at a youth club were given a musical instrument.
This bar chart shows the number of children given each type of instrument.

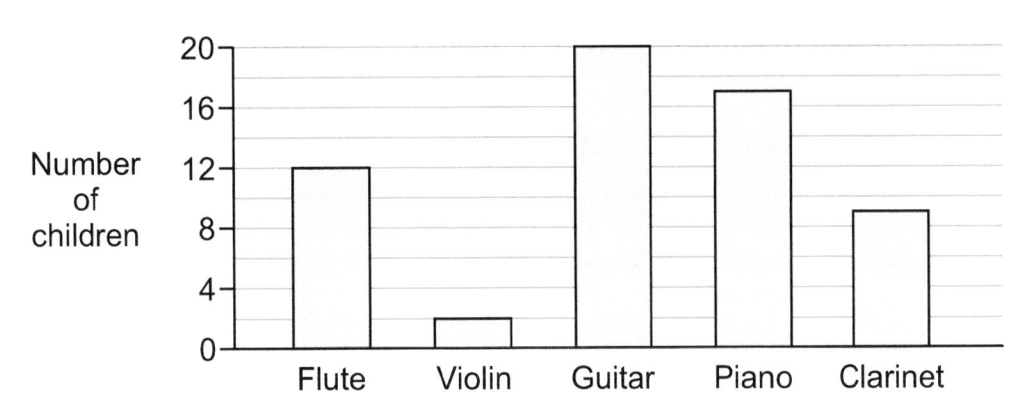

a) How many children were given a clarinet?

b) A total of 75 children attend the youth club.
How many children were not given an instrument?

7) Asha makes the shape below from cube blocks.
She paints the outside of the shape purple.

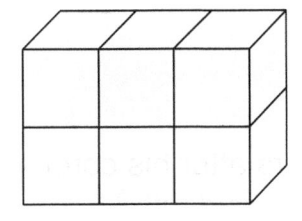

How many cube faces will be painted purple?

20   19   22   11   13
☐   ☐   ☐   ☐   ☐

Go to the next question

8) The River Rhine is 766 miles long.
The River Thames is 215 miles long.

What is the total length of the two rivers to the nearest 10 miles?

☐☐☐☐ miles

9) The table below gives information about some kings and queens of England.

	Year of coronation	Year of death	Number of husbands/wives
William I	1066	?	1
Henry VIII	1509	1547	6
Elizabeth I	1559	1603	0
Charles II	1661	1685	1

a) How many fewer wives did Charles II have than Henry VIII?

6 ☐   5 ☐   2 ☐   1 ☐   0 ☐

b) William I died 21 years after his coronation.
What was the year of his death?

☐☐☐☐

c) How many years were there between
Elizabeth I's coronation and her death?

☐☐☐

10 The trophy cabinet in Shobna's school has 7 shelves.
There are 5 trophies on each shelf and each trophy has 2 handles.

a) How many handles are there in the trophy cabinet?

b) $\frac{2}{5}$ of the trophies are silver.
How many silver trophies are there in the cabinet?

11 Which of these shapes has exactly 3 lines of symmetry?

A   B   C   D   E

12 What is 16 × 0?

1   60   0   160   16

13 Which of these is the best estimate for the weight of a hen's egg?

5.5 kg   55 g   55 kg   550 g   5.5 g

Go to the next question

14) Elijah, Selwyn, Varesh and Jackie are doing a science experiment.
They each put a plant in water and count the number of bubbles that they see.
Their results are shown in this pictogram.

Elijah	◯ ◯
Selwyn	◯ ◯ ◯
Varesh	◯ ◯ ◯ ◯ ◯
Jackie	◯ ◯ ◯ ◖

◯ = 4 bubbles

a) How many fewer bubbles than Jackie did Elijah see?

b) How many bubbles were seen in total?

c) What fraction of all the bubbles were from Selwyn's experiment?

$\frac{3}{14}$ $\frac{12}{42}$ $\frac{12}{14}$ $\frac{3}{11}$ $\frac{12}{54}$

(15) Grant has put some shapes into this sorting diagram.

	Contains an acute angle	Contains no acute angles
All sides the same length	A △	B ⬠
Sides different lengths	C	D

Each section of the diagram has been labelled with a letter.

a) Which section of the diagram would this shape go into?

    A   B   C   D
    ☐   ☐   ☐   ☐

b) Which section of the diagram would a scalene triangle go into?

    A   B   C   D
    ☐   ☐   ☐   ☐

(16) Which number is exactly halfway between 6.5 and 9.5?

    7.5   8   9   8.5   7
    ☐   ☐   ☐   ☐   ☐

Go to the next question ⇨

17) Brendan posts a letter to his friend who lives abroad.
The letter takes 3 weeks and 4 days to arrive.

a) How long did the letter take to arrive in days?

☐☐ days

b) Brendan posted the letter on Monday.
On what day of the week did the letter arrive?

Friday ☐   Tuesday ☐   Thursday ☐   Saturday ☐   Monday ☐

18) The lunch menu at a café is shown below.

Meals		Drinks	
Chicken stew	£8.10	Orange juice	95 p
Vegetable lasagne	£6.40	Mineral water	60 p
Jacket potato	£4.85		

a) How many different combinations of a meal and a drink are there?

3 ☐   6 ☐   5 ☐   9 ☐   4 ☐

b) Monica chooses the vegetable lasagne and orange juice.
She pays with a £20 note. How much change does she receive?

£ ☐☐.☐☐

19) A building set contains 600 pieces.
Mr Martin buys a set for each of his nine grandchildren.
How many pieces does he buy in total?

20) Two shapes (A and B) and a point (P) have been drawn on this grid.

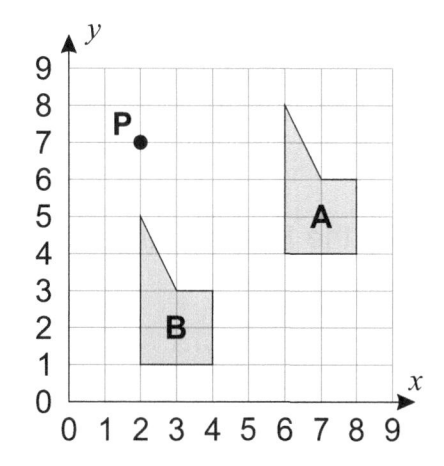

a) B is a translation of A. Which of these describes the translation?

☐ 3 squares left, 3 squares down

☐ 4 squares right, 3 squares down

☐ 4 squares left, 3 squares down

☐ 3 squares right, 4 squares up

☐ 4 squares left, 3 squares up

b) P is translated three squares right and one square down.
What are the new coordinates of P?

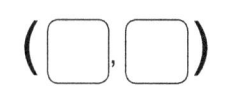

21) Taylor sees a lion at a safari park that weighs 174 kg.
Taylor's kitten weighs 100 times less than the lion.

a) How much does Taylor's kitten weigh?

   17.4 kg   174 g   0.174 kg   1.74 kg   17.4 g
   ☐   ☐   ☐   ☐   ☐

b) Taylor also sees a giraffe that weighs 1033 kg.
How many kilograms heavier than the lion is the giraffe?

☐☐☐☐ kg

22) What number is shown by the Roman numeral below?

XLIX

   26   69   71   51   49
   ☐   ☐   ☐   ☐   ☐

23) Miley's hair is 36 cm long.
Quinn's hair is 57 mm long.

a) What is the difference between Miley and Quinn's hair lengths?

   21 mm   303 cm   293 mm   21 cm   303 mm
   ☐   ☐   ☐   ☐   ☐

b) How long is Quinn's hair to the nearest centimetre?

☐☐☐ cm

24) Kamal and Brandi have created this number machine.

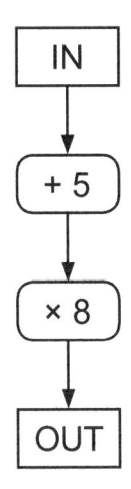

```
  IN
   ↓
  +5
   ↓
  ×8
   ↓
  OUT
```

a) Kamal puts 4 into the machine. What number comes out?

b) Brandi gets 88 out of the number machine. What number did she put in?

25) $5/12$ of Ranj's video games are action games.
$1/12$ of his video games are puzzle games.
What fraction of Ranj's games are not action or puzzle games?

$4/12$ $1/2$ $5/12$ $1/6$ $1/3$

Go to the next question

26) A greengrocer plots the number of carrots she has in stock every hour. She receives a delivery of carrots once a day.

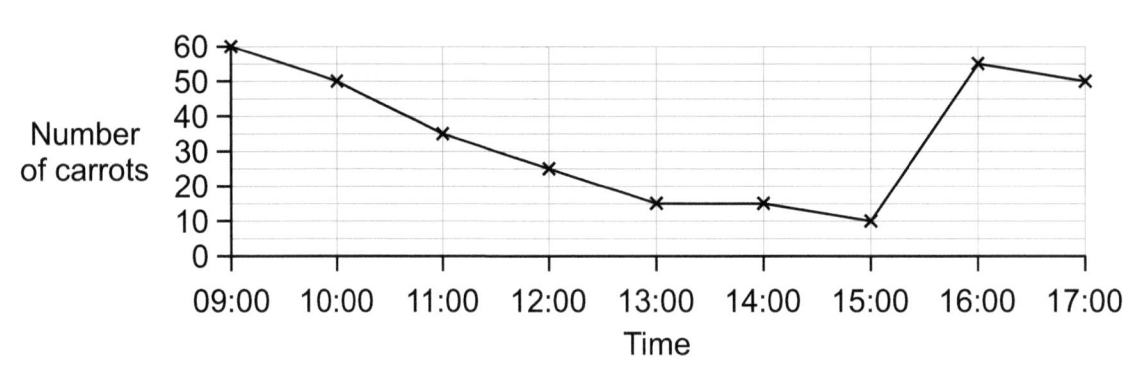

a) How many carrots did the greengrocer sell between 10 am and 1 pm?

b) In which hour did the greengrocer receive a delivery of carrots?

09:00 - 10:00   12:00 - 13:00   14:00 - 15:00   15:00 - 16:00   16:00 - 17:00
☐   ☐   ☐   ☐   ☐

27) There are 154 desks in a school. Each desk has 4 chairs around it.

a) How many chairs are there around the desks in total?

b) Half of the desks have wooden legs.
How many of the desks have wooden legs?

c) There are 14 classrooms in the school.
Each classroom contains the same number of desks.
What is the total number of desks in one classroom?

28 These are the ingredients needed to make 8 glasses of a fruit drink.

> 2 watermelons
> 250 ml lemon juice
> 100 g sugar
> 1 litre fizzy water
> 1 lime

a) How many millilitres of lemon juice would you need to make 4 glasses of the drink?

☐☐☐☐ ml

b) How many whole limes would you need to make 21 glasses of the drink?

☐

c) How much fizzy water would you need to make 12 glasses of the drink?

15 000 ml	2 litres	1500 ml	1.25 litres	500 ml
☐	☐	☐	☐	☐

29) 36 people were asked if they would rather go on holiday in the UK or abroad.
Their answers are shown in the diagram below.
Each section represents the fraction of the people who were asked.

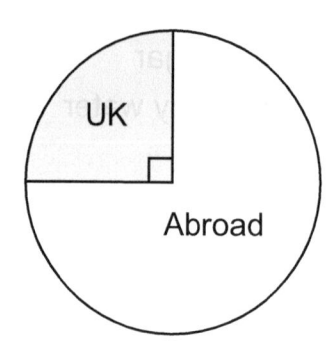

How many people said they would rather go on holiday in the UK?

☐☐

30) Toilet rolls can be bought in three different pack sizes.

| 4-pack £2.40 | 9-pack £4.50 | 12-pack £9.60 |

a) What is the cheapest possible price you can pay for 36 toilet rolls?

£☐☐.☐☐

b) A new multi-pack goes on sale that costs ⅔ of the price of the 9-pack.
How much does this new multi-pack cost?

£☐☐.☐☐

Stop — you may check your answers in this section only

CGP

11+ Practice Papers

For the **CEM** test

Answer Book

Ages 8-9

Set A — Paper 1

Section 1: Verbal Reasoning — Comprehension

1) B
Lines 2-3 state that there are "children dressed up as monsters" on Halloween, which is one of the reasons the writer gives for it being the spookiest night of the year.

2) A
Lines 13 states that the Otherworld was said to be "the realm of spirits". A 'realm' means a kingdom, so the Celts believed that this is where the spirits lived.

3) D
Lines 15-16 state that the Celts "may have sacrificed cattle and crops" to "please the spirits".

4) B
Lines 17-20 state that one of the activities "on this night" (31st October) was "choosing a nut to roast on the fire".

5) D
Line 11 states that Samhain was celebrated on "31st October", and line 25 states that "All Hallows' Day" is "celebrated on 1st November", which is the day after.

6) B
Lines 23-24 state that "Celtic traditions like Samhain began to fall out of favour", which means that Celtic traditions weren't as popular.

7) B
Line 34 states that the people who answered their doors "asked the soulers to pray for the souls of their relatives", not that the soulers themselves asked people to pray for them.

8) C
Lines 35-36 state that the "tradition of souling" moved away from its roots and "evolved into the trick-or-treating that is often practised on Halloween today."

9) A
Lines 38-40 state that "Halloween's popularity in the British Isles dwindled" as celebrations like "Guy Fawkes Night" were introduced.

10) D
Line 42 states that at first "Halloween was only celebrated in some Southern United States".

11) D
Lines 43-45 state that "Halloween's popularity increased in the United States" when "a large number of Irish and Scottish immigrants moved there."

12) B
Line 36 states that "trick-or-treating" is "often practised on Halloween today", and lines 50-51 state that having "houses covered with gruesome decorations" is also currently a "popular part" of Halloween.

13) C
Lines 55-56 state that "In 2017, it was estimated that £25 million would be spent in Britain on pumpkin carving alone."

14) C
Lines 45-47 describe popular Halloween activities in the United States in the 1900s, line 50 states that "horror films" are popular during Halloween, and lines 51-53 state that "Halloween in the UK" has become "increasingly similar to the celebrations in the United States." However, the amount spent on Halloween costumes is not mentioned.

15) B
In lines 56-57, the writer states that Halloween has become "larger and more spectacular", and that it is "hard to imagine" the "simpler beginnings" of Halloween. This suggests that they think it has changed a lot since it was first celebrated.

16) A
"numerous" means 'several' or 'various'.

17) B
"brought about" means 'caused' or 'led to', so the phrase means that new traditions started.

18) A
"evolved" means 'developed or changed over time'.

19) C
"dwindled" means 'became smaller' or 'declined'.

20) D
"gruesome" means 'frightening' or 'horrible'.

Section 2: Verbal Reasoning — Synonyms

1) sip
Both words mean 'to take in liquid'.

2) healthy
Both words mean 'in good physical condition'.

3) complain
Both words mean 'to moan'.

4) finish
Both words mean 'to conclude'.

5) celebrated
Both words mean 'well known'.

6) tasty
Both words mean 'having a pleasant flavour'.

7) chat
Both words mean 'a talk'.

8) loot
Both words mean 'to take without permission'.

9) shatter
Both words mean 'to separate into pieces'.

10) peaceful
Both words mean 'tranquil'.

11) sickness
Both words mean 'ill health'.

12) clutch
Both words mean 'to take and hold something firmly'.

13) shut
Both words mean 'to cover or seal'.

14) student
Both words mean 'someone who learns through studying'.

15) complicated
Both words mean 'difficult'.

16) fix
Both words mean 'to mend'.

Section 3: Verbal Reasoning — Antonyms

1) fake
'real' means 'genuine', whereas 'fake' means 'false'.

2) hilly
'flat' means 'level and smooth', whereas 'hilly' means 'bumpy and uneven'.

3) guilty
'innocent' means 'not having committed a wrongdoing', whereas 'guilty' means 'having committed a wrongdoing'.

4) bought
'sold' means 'gave away in exchange for money', whereas 'bought' means 'received in exchange for money'.

5) leave
'arrive' means 'to come to a place', whereas 'leave' means 'to go away from a place'.

6) question
'answer' means 'a solution or response', whereas 'question' means 'a problem or query'.

7) truth
'lie' means 'something that is false', whereas 'truth' means 'something that is correct'.

8) fresh
'rotten' means 'decayed', whereas 'fresh' means 'newly produced'.

9) messy
'tidy' means 'orderly', whereas 'messy' means 'disorderly'.

10) straight
'bent' means 'curved or twisted', whereas 'straight' means 'not having curves or twists'.

11) danger
'safety' means 'protection from harm', whereas 'danger' means 'the possibility of harm'.

12) entrance
'exit' means 'the way out', whereas 'entrance' means 'the way in'.

13) whole
'piece' means 'a part', whereas 'whole' means 'the entirety'.

14) reject
'accept' means 'to allow', whereas 'reject' means 'to deny'.

Section 4: Verbal Reasoning — Related Words

1) medal
All the words are examples of prizes.

2) Italian
All the words are examples of languages.

3) Oxford
All the words are names of English cities.

4) freezing
All the words mean 'cold'.

5) choir
All the words are examples of musical groups.

6) superb
All the words mean 'really good'.

7) pie
All the words are examples of main meals.

8) haddock
All the words are types of fish.

9) thumb
All the words are parts of a hand.

10) coop
All the words are examples of animal enclosures.

11) mustard
All the words are examples of savoury condiments.

12) Africa
All the words are continents on Earth.

13) clown
All the words are types of people who make others laugh.

14) journey
All the words refer to a period of travel.

15) decade
All the words are measurements of time.

Section 5: Numerical Reasoning

1) 6
$4 \times 6 = 24$, so $24 \div 4 = 6$.

2) 4
Saleem flipped the coin $8 + 3 = 11$ times.
Clive flipped the coin $6 + 9 = 15$ times.
So Saleem flipped the coin $15 - 11 = 4$ fewer times than Clive.

3) 1476
In figures, one thousand is 1000, four hundred is 400 and seventy-six is 76. Adding them gives 1476.

4) 10 cm²
There are 9 whole squares shaded and 2 half squares shaded, so the area of the shape is $9 + ½ + ½ = 10$ cm².

5) scalene
Go through each option to decide which is the right answer. All equilateral and isosceles triangles have at least two equal sides (equilateral triangles have three). Right-angled triangles have one 90° angle, but the other two angles could be the same (45°), which would give an isosceles triangle (see above). A scalene triangle has three different side lengths, so Emlyn's triangle cannot be scalene.

6) 5
Each full symbol on the pictogram = 2 pins.
Each half symbol = $2 \div 2 = 1$ pin.
For Evan, five whole symbols = $5 \times 2 = 10$ pins.
For Nilesh, two whole symbols = $2 \times 2 = 4$ pins and one half symbol = 1 pin, so Nilesh knocked down $4 + 1 = 5$ pins.
So Evan knocked down $10 - 5 = 5$ more pins than Nilesh.

7) 0.27
In figures, two tenths is 0.2 and seven hundredths is 0.07. Adding them gives 0.27.

8) 8632
To make the largest number possible, put the digits in order with the largest first, giving 8632.

9) −1

Each term is decreasing by 3 (11 − 8 = 3, 8 − 5 = 3 and 5 − 2 = 3). So the number that goes in the box must be 2 − 3 = −1.

10) 15:47

The time shown on the clock is forty-seven minutes past three, so is 3:47. Latisha is having afternoon tea, so the time must be 3:47 pm. Add 12 to 3 to get the time on the 24-hour clock, which is 15:47.

11) (1, 5)

Draw the final corner of the square as shown below.
Reading off the coordinates of this corner gives (1, 5).

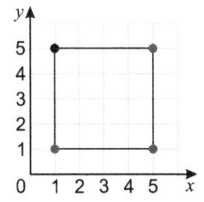

12) 2250 g

The pointer is one quarter of the way between 2 kg and 3 kg, so the weight in kg is 2.25 kg. 1 kg = 1000 g, so the weight in grams is 2.25 × 1000 = 2250 g.

13) 0.75

³⁄₄ is the same as 0.75.

14) £9.75

To find out how much Katya has after buying the book, partition £4.25 into £4 and 25p, and subtract each from £12:
£12 − £4 = £8 and £8 − 25p = £7.75.
Then add on the £2 her grandad gave her: £7.75 + £2 = £9.75.

15) 216

Reuel has 72 × 3 stamps. To do this multiplication, partition 72 into 70 and 2, and multiply each part separately by 3.
For 70 × 3, you know 7 × 3 = 21. 70 is 10 times bigger than 7, so 70 × 3 = 21 × 10 = 210.
2 × 3 = 6, so 72 × 3 = 210 + 6 = 216.

16) 6

9 (3 × 3), 18 (6 × 3) and 6 (2 × 3) are multiples of 3.
4 and 6 are factors of 24, since 4 × 6 = 24.
The '?' is in the part of the diagram where the circles overlap, so it must represent a number that's both a multiple of 3 and a factor of 24. So 6 is the only option that can replace the '?'.

Section 6: Non-Verbal Reasoning

1) D

Option A is the wrong shape. Option B has the wrong shading. Option C is a 180 degree rotation.

2) C

Option A has the wrong shading. Option B is a 180 degree rotation. In option D, one of the small black squares is in the wrong place.

3) B

Option A is a 135 degree clockwise rotation. In option C, the shape at the front has not been reflected. In option D, the shape at the front is the wrong shape.

4) D

In option A, the line with the circle has not been reflected. In option B, the bars have not been reflected and they have the wrong shading. Option C has the wrong shading.

5) C

In each series square, the triangle rotates 180 degrees. The shading of the triangle alternates between white and black.

6) A

In each series square, the triangle at the front moves to the back. The shading of the triangles stays the same.

7) A

In each series square, one candle disappears and the remaining candles rotate 90 degrees clockwise.

8) C

In each series square, the shaded rectangles alternate between grey and black. One more small white rectangle is added onto each of the large rectangles on either side of the figure.

9) D

In each series square, the black star moves one place along the line, working from the bottom end of the line to the top end. The white star moves one place along the line, working from the top end of the line to the bottom end.

10) A

All figures must contain two identical shapes on the same side of a line. Both shapes must have the same shading.

11) D

In all figures, the shape on the left must have a solid outline. The shape on the right must have a dashed outline and be a squashed version of the shape on the left.

12) D

In all figures, all of the frog's feet must be the same shape as the shape on its chest. The shading of the frog's two middle feet must match the shading of the frog's eyes.

13) B

In all figures, the shape on the right of the grid must have one more side than the shape on the left.

14) C

All figures must have three shapes that are identical apart from shading. The shape at the front must be pointing left, the shape in the middle must be pointing up, and the shape at the back must be pointing right.

Set A — Paper 2

Section 1: Numerical Reasoning

1 a) Angles Q and S are acute

An acute angle is less than 90° and an obtuse angle is bigger than 90° but less than 180°. Q and S are acute, P is a right angle and R is obtuse, so only the fourth option is correct.

1 b) P

A right angle is 90°.

2 a) 4

Using the times tables you know that 12 × 4 = 48, so Sundeep plants 48 ÷ 12 = 4 seeds in each pot.

2 b) 4

48 = 50 − 2, so 3 × 48 = 50 × 3 − 2 × 3 = 150 − 6 = 144.
There aren't quite enough seeds in 3 packs, so Carla will need to buy 4 packs.

3 a) 25
There are 12 marks for right-handed boys and 13 marks for right-handed girls. 12 + 13 = 25.

3 b) 4/16
There are 4 marks for left-handed boys and 12 marks for right-handed boys, so there are 4 + 12 = 16 boys in total. As a fraction, the number of boys that are left-handed is 4/16.

4 a) 69
The first two odd numbers in the list are 3 and 23. To multiply these numbers, partition 23 into 20 and 3, and multiply each part separately: 20 × 3 = 60, 3 × 3 = 9, so 23 × 3 = 60 + 9 = 69.

4 b) 105
45 (5 × 9) and 60 (5 × 12) are the only multiples of 5 in the list. 45 + 60 = 105.

4 c) 60 − 32 > 45 − 23
'>' means more than. 60 − 32 = 28 and 45 − 23 = 22. 28 > 22, so 60 − 32 > 45 − 23 is true.

5 a) 456
Partition 912 into 900 and 12, and divide each part by 2: 900 ÷ 2 = 450, 12 ÷ 2 = 6, so 912 ÷ 2 = 450 + 6 = 456.

5 b) 1432
First add the extra 640 books to 912. Partition 640 into 600 and 40 and add them separately: 912 + 600 = 1512 and 1512 + 40 = 1552.
You then need to subtract the books donated. Partition 120 into 100 and 20 and subtract each part separately: 1552 − 100 = 1452 and 1452 − 20 = 1432.

6 a) white
'White' is the third highest bar on the chart.

6 b) 34
Add up the number of cars that are not blue: 11 + 10 + 4 + 9 = 34 cars.

6 c) £35.00
There are 4 + 10 = 14 red and black cars, so you need to multiply £2.50 by 14: £2.50 × 10 = £25 and £2.50 × 4 = £10, so £2.50 × 14 = £25 + £10 = £35.

7 a) 3
A regular polygon has equal side lengths. The first shape (square), second shape (regular pentagon) and the fifth shape (regular hexagon) have equal side lengths. The third shape (irregular hexagon) and fourth shape (isosceles triangle) do not.

7 b) 2/5
A hexagon has 6 sides, so there are 2 hexagons (third and fifth shapes). So 2 out of 5 or 2/5 of the shapes are hexagons.

8 a) 8:55 am
The time shown on the clock is 5 minutes past 7 and you know the time is in the morning, so it's 7:05 am. Counting on 1 hour and 50 minutes from this time gives you the time Rachel finished her run. 1 hour later than 7:05 am is 8:05 am and 50 minutes later than 8:05 am is 8:55 am.

8 b) 11 minutes
1 hour 50 minutes = 60 + 50 = 110 minutes. Divide this by 10 to find 1/10: 110 ÷ 10 = 11 minutes.

9 a) 100
Oti has £10 and magazines cost 10p. 10p goes into £1 ten times, so with £10 Oti could buy 10 × 10 = 100 magazines.

9 b) £3.75
A hardback cost £2.50 and three paperbacks cost £1.25 × 3 = £3.75. So Oti spent: £2.50 + £3.75 = £6.25 and got £10 − £6.25 = £3.75 change.

10 a) E
Amelia's shape is divided into 8 equal parts. 4 out of 8 parts are shaded, which is equivalent to half of the shape. Half of shape E is also shaded.

10 b) 3
There are 4 lines of symmetry as shown here:

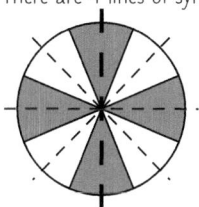

Amelia has already drawn the line shown in bold, so there are 4 − 1 = 3 more lines to be drawn.

11 a) 400 m
Change one of the units so both distances are in m or km — m are easier to use here. To convert km to m you multiply by 1000, so 1.8 km is 1800 m. 1800 m − 1400 m = 400 m.

11 b) 1439 m
To become 1400 m when rounded to the nearest hundred, the distance must be bigger than or equal to 1350 m and less than 1450 m. This is only true for 1439 m.

12 a) £4.50
5 × 9 = 45. 90 is 10 times bigger than 9, so 5p × 90 = 45 × 10 = 450p which is the same as £4.50.

12 b) 30
2/3 of the stickers are purple, so 1 − 2/3 = 1/3 of the stickers are not purple. 1/3 of 90 is 90 ÷ 3 = 30.

12 c) 42 cm
The perimeter of the shape is made up of six 3 cm lengths and six 4 cm lengths. 3 × 6 = 18 and 4 × 6 = 24, so the perimeter is 18 + 24 = 42 cm.

13 a) 0.46 m
Luke is the tallest with a height of 1.65 m.
Bill is the shortest with a height of 1.19 m.
Subtract Bill's height from Luke's height:
```
  1.⁵6̸¹5
− 1.1 9
  0.4 6
```

13 b) 183 cm
Change Manon's height to centimetres:
1 m = 100 cm, so 1.47 m = 1.47 × 100 = 147 cm.
Add on 36 cm using the column method:
```
  1 4 7
+   3 6
  1 8 3
      1
```

13 c) 8
Aziz's height is 1.2 m. Try multiplying 1.2 m by different numbers to see how many times it goes into 10 m. Using the times tables, you know 12 × 8 = 96. 1.2 is 10 times smaller than 12, so 1.2 m × 8 = 9.6 m. You also know 12 × 9 = 108, so 1.2 m × 9 = 10.8 m. This is too big, so Aziz's height can fit into the height of his house 8 whole times.

Section 2: Verbal Reasoning — Cloze

1) occur
'The modern Paralympics **occur** every four years'

2) television
'The London 2012 Paralympics were watched on **television**'

3) major
'the Paralympics haven't always been such a **major** sporting event.'

4) history
'the Olympics have a long **history**'

5) recent
'the Paralympics are a more **recent** development.'

6) soldiers
'Guttmann began working with **soldiers** with spinal injuries'

7) recover
'which involved helping them to **recover**'

8) popular
'This proved so **popular** that in 1948, Guttmann organised'

9) involved
'This event, which **involved** an archery competition'

10) wheelchairs
'an archery competition for athletes in **wheelchairs**'

11) became
'These later **became** known as the Paralympics'

12) expanded
'The event has **expanded** over time'

13) range
'so that athletes with a wider **range** of disabilities can compete.'

14) grown
'The number of sports included has also **grown**'

15) important
'The Paralympic Games play an **important** role'

16) continue
'the Paralympics **continue** to grow in popularity'

Section 3: Non-Verbal Reasoning

1) B
The figure moves up and a copy appears below it.

2) A
The smaller shape is copied onto each corner of the large shape.

3) D
The outline of the shape becomes solid. A small square with a dashed outline appears inside the shape.

4) B
The figure rotates 90 degrees clockwise. Two arrows appear, which both point towards the right.

5) B
The line becomes thicker, and half of the shapes move to the other side of the line.

6) D
The figure is reflected across. The mug and the oval swap patterns.

7) D
Another identical shape is added to the end of the bug's body. The bug's head moves behind its body.

8) C
All figures must contain a hatched shape in front of a black shape.

9) A
All figures must be identical apart from rotation.

10) A
All figures must contain three different shapes which each have a different shading.

11) B
In all figures, the shading on the mouse's nose must match the shading on the inside of the mouse's ears. The mouse must have a pointed face.

12) C
All figures must contain two small shapes in front of a large shape which has a dashed outline. The number of sides of the large shape must be one more than the number of sides on each of the small shapes.

13) B
In all figures, moving from top to bottom, the length of the rectangles must increase and the number of vertical black lines inside each rectangle must increase by one.

14) C
Working from left to right, the black shape becomes grey.

15) C
Working from left to right, the number of points on the star decreases by one. The number of dashed lines also decreases by one.

16) D
Working from top to bottom, the number of identical socks increases by one. The new sock is added on top of the previous sock.

17) D
Working from left to right, one more shape is shaded. The shapes are shaded in order of size, from the largest to the smallest.

18) D
Working from left to right, the arrow moves to point at a different shape, going in the order: black, grey, white. The style of arrowhead is the same in each column.

19) A
Working from left to right, the figure rotates 45 degrees clockwise. The black shape moves further along the white rectangle.

20) B
Working from top to bottom, a smaller version of the large shape appears inside the large shape. The new shape has a dashed outline. The shading of the teardrop changes from white to grey to black.

21) C
The figure is rotated 90 degrees clockwise. Options A and D are the wrong shape. Option B has the wrong shading.

22) A
The figure is rotated 135 degrees clockwise. Option B has the wrong shading. Option C is the wrong shape. Option D is a rotated reflection.

23) C
The figure is rotated 90 degrees clockwise. Options A and D are the wrong shape. Option B is a reflection.

24) D
The figure is rotated 90 degrees anticlockwise. In option A, the grey stripe is in the wrong place. Option B has triangles instead of circles. In option C, the shading of the circles is wrong.

25) C
The figure is rotated 45 degrees clockwise. Option A is a rotated reflection. Option B has the wrong shading. In option D, the black rectangles and the three white squares next to them are in the wrong place.

26) C
The figure is rotated 90 degrees clockwise. Option A is a rotated reflection. In option B, the spiral is going in the wrong direction. In option D, the spiral is the wrong shape.

27) B
The figure is rotated 180 degrees. In option A, the shading is wrong. In options C and D, the layering is wrong.

28) B
All other figures contain only one type of shading.

29) D
In all other figures, the head of the snake is pointing to the right.

30) D
In all other figures, the circle and the triangle are on the same side of the dividing line.

31) A
In all other figures, the tallest tree is on the left-hand side.

32) C
All other figures contain five black diamonds.

33) E
All other figures are identical apart from shading and rotation.

34) C
In all other figures, the shading of the car's front wheel matches the shading of its windows.

Set B — Paper 1

Section 1: Verbal Reasoning — Comprehension 1

1) B
The phrase 'to watch the world go by' means 'to watch people living their normal lives'.

2) C
In line 2, the road below Sarah's window is described as a "busy high street".

3) B
Lines 18-19 state that the toy shop was full of "all sorts of strange" things. This means that the shop sold unusual toys.

4) A
The phrase 'to pale in comparison to' means 'to look worse when compared to'. So the other toys in the shop didn't seem as good once Sarah had seen the kite.

5) C
Line 22 states that the kite was "enormous".

6) D
Lines 26-28 state that Sarah "volunteered for extra chores" so that "she could save as much money as possible." This suggests that her parents gave her more pocket money for doing extra chores.

7) D
The text mentions that Sarah is looking out of her window on the Saturday the "week before her birthday" (line 34), but the actual date of her birthday is not given.

8) C
Lines 30-31 state that "the wait until" Sarah's birthday "seemed impossible", which shows that Sarah feels that it is a long time to wait. She shows her impatience by counting down the days on her calendar to check how many days are left until her birthday.

9) C
Line 35 states that it was "a miserable, rainy, dark day" when Sarah saw the mysterious person go into the toy shop. The mysterious person was also carrying "an enormous umbrella" and "jumping to avoid the puddles forming on the pavement" (lines 39-40).

10) B
Lines 50-51 state that "a gust of wind caught the person's umbrella and Sarah was able to see the face that had been hidden underneath it." The face that she sees is her dad's and she recognises him at once.

11) C
Lines 55-56 explain how Sarah realised that "she was going to get the kite for her birthday after all." This shows that her dad bought the kite as a birthday present for Sarah. Putting your finger to your lips suggests that something is a secret. Sarah's dad put his finger to his lips because it was still a week before her birthday and she wasn't supposed to know about the present yet.

12) D
'relieved' means 'no longer worried'. Earlier in the text, Sarah was worried because she saw someone else buying the kite she wanted. When she realised it was her dad and that he had bought the kite for her, a "grin spread across her face" (line 55). This shows that she was no longer worried because she realised she would get the kite after all.

13) B
"watchful" means 'observant' or 'attentive'.

14) A
"glinted" means 'sparkled' or 'twinkled'.

15) C
The phrase 'to long for something' means 'to wish you had something'. Sarah gazed at the kite "longingly", which means that she wished she had the kite.

Section 2: Verbal Reasoning — Comprehension 2

1) B
Lines 1-2 state that the "three enormous waterfalls" are "known collectively as Niagara Falls." This means that Niagara Falls is a group of three waterfalls.

2) C
Lines 6 states that "Angel Falls in Venezuela is widely accepted as the world's tallest waterfall."

3) D
Line 15 states that Annie Edson Taylor "went over the Falls" in 1901.

4) D
Line 15 states that Annie Edson Taylor "went over the Falls in a barrel", so she didn't use a special boat.

5) B
Line 17 states that Annie was "very bruised and frightened". 'Frightened' means 'unnerved' or 'shaken'.

6) C
Lines 22-24 state that Charles Blondin "performed a whole range of unbelievable stunts" including "crossing the tightrope" while "wearing stilts."

7) A
Lines 26-27 state that "Millions of people visit Niagara Falls each year to admire the amazing views", which means that they come to look at the scenery.

8) C
Lines 27-28 state that the "Maid of the Mist" is a "well-known boat tour" used by tourists who wish to "see the waterfalls close up."

9) D
"surging" means 'gushing' or 'rushing'.

10) B
"astonishingly" means 'incredibly' or 'surprisingly'.

Section 3: Verbal Reasoning — Odd One Out

1) sharp
The other three mean 'quick'.

2) hammered
The other three are tools.

3) nose
The other three are parts of a foot.

4) supermarket
The other three are names of people who work in shops.

5) Multiplication
The other three are subjects taught at school.

6) London
The other three are countries.

7) water
The other three can be used to mark surfaces and create pictures.

8) go-kart
The other three can be found in a playground.

9) arm
The other three are body parts that humans don't have.

10) cycle
The other three are activities that you don't necessarily need equipment to do.

11) America
The other three are all oceans.

12) poster
The other three are examples of books.

13) doormat
The other three are things you could hang on the wall.

14) neighbour
The other three mean 'friend'.

15) saucepan
The other three are all electrical kitchen appliances.

16) entertainment
The other three mean 'comical'.

17) chop
The other three are cooking techniques that involve heat.

18) outstanding
The other three mean 'strange'.

Section 4: Verbal Reasoning — Shuffled Sentences

1) waiting
The words can be rearranged into the sentence 'She sprinted down the long path.'

2) performed
The words can be rearranged into the sentence 'The actor couldn't remember his lines.'

3) terrify
The words can be rearranged into the sentence 'The mansion is haunted by ghosts.'

4) threat
The words can be rearranged into the sentence 'Not all snakes are poisonous.'

5) played
The words can be rearranged into the sentence 'Satoshi loved to collect trading cards.'

6) like
The words can be rearranged into the sentence 'Joel hated mushrooms on his pizza.'

7) taste
The words can be rearranged into the sentence 'Sugary sweets are bad for your teeth.'

8) finish
The words can be rearranged into the sentence 'Millie was stuck on the final puzzle.'

9) tyre
The words can be rearranged into the sentence 'He drove the car very slowly.'

10) fought
The words can be rearranged into the sentence 'The brothers looked very similar.'

11) stripes
The words can be rearranged into the sentence 'My sock has a hole in it.'

12) people
The words can be rearranged into the sentence 'Public speaking made her nervous.'

13) bed
The words can be rearranged into the sentence 'My best friend is sleeping over tonight.'

14) cackle
The words can be rearranged into the sentence 'Zara told many hilarious jokes at dinner.'

15) visited
The words can be rearranged into the sentence 'Nathan started to miss his family.'

Section 5: Verbal Reasoning — Cloze

1) heard
'Have you ever **heard** the expression "dead as a dodo"?'

2) has
'the dodo, which **has** been extinct'

3) over
'for **over** 300 years.'

4) means
'This **means** that there aren't any dodos still alive'

5) lived
'They **lived** on the island of Mauritius'

6) coast
'off the east **coast** of Africa.'

7) arrived
'Until humans **arrived** on Mauritius in the 1500s'

8) able
'dodos were **able** to survive with no natural predators'

9) change
'things started to **change**.'

10) Although
'**Although** people did hunt some of the dodos'

11) believed
'it is **believed** that'

12) threat
'the biggest **threat** to dodos came from the animals'

13) brought
'that people had **brought** with them'

14) including
'These animals, **including** pigs and rats'

15) lot
'stole a **lot** of their food.'

16) many
'there weren't **many** dodos left alive.'

17) alive
'there weren't many dodos left **alive**.'

18) exactly
'Nobody knows **exactly** when the last dodo died'

Section 6: Non-Verbal Reasoning

1) B
There should be a dark grey block, two cubes long, at the back of the figure. This rules out options A, C and D.

2) A
There should be a block, two cubes long, lying along the bottom of the figure. This rules out options C and D. There should be a cube at the top left-hand side of the figure, which rules out option B.

3) A
There should be a dark grey block, two cubes tall, on the right-hand side of the figure. This rules out options B and D. There should be a cube at the front of the figure on the left-hand side at the top, which rules out option C.

4) D
There should be a dark grey cube at the bottom of the figure on the left-hand side. This rules out options B and C. There should be a block, two cubes long, coming out of the page on the right-hand side of the figure. This rules out option A.

5) C
There should be a block, three cubes long, at the back of the figure. This rules out options A and D. There should be a cube at the front of the figure on the right-hand side, which rules out option B.

6) D
There should be a cube at the bottom of the figure, in the middle. This rules out options A, B and C.

7) D
In options A and C, the fold line has moved. In option B, the figure has been broken apart along the fold line.

8) B
In options A and D, the part of the figure that has been folded is the wrong shape. In option C, the fold line has moved.

9) C
In option A, the part of the figure originally to the right of the fold line should still be visible. In option B, the part of the figure originally to the right of the fold line is the wrong shape. In option D, the fold line has moved.

10) C
In options A and B, the fold line has moved. In option D, the part of the figure originally below the fold line should still be visible.

11) A
In option B, the part of the figure originally to the left of the fold line is the wrong shape. In option C, the part of the figure that has been folded is the wrong shape. In option D, the fold line has moved.

12) C
In options A and D, the part of the figure that has been folded is the wrong shape. In option B, the fold line has moved.

13) B
In option A, the part of the figure that has been folded is the wrong shape. In option C, the fold line has moved. In option D, the part of the figure originally to the left of the fold line is the wrong shape.

14) D
There are four blocks visible from above, which rules out options A and C. There are two blocks visible on the right, which rules out option B.

15) A
There are three blocks visible from above, which rules out options B and D. There is one block visible on the right, which rules out option C.

16) B
There are six blocks visible from above, which rules out options C and D. There are two blocks visible on the left, which rules out option A.

17) A
There are four blocks visible from above, which rules out options C and D. There are two blocks visible at the front, which rules out option B.

18) C
There are five blocks visible from above, which rules out options B and D. There are two blocks visible at the back, which rules out option A.

19) **D**
There are five blocks visible from above, which rules out options A and C. There are three blocks visible on the left, which rules out option B.

Set B — Paper 2

Section 1: Verbal Reasoning — Antonyms

1) delay
'hurry' means 'to make quicker', whereas 'delay' means 'to make slower'.

2) definitely
'maybe' means 'possibly', whereas 'definitely' means 'certainly'.

3) soothe
'irritate' means 'to cause discomfort', whereas 'soothe' means 'to ease discomfort'.

4) unnecessary
'crucial' means 'very important', whereas 'unnecessary' means 'not important'.

5) push
'drag' means 'to pull something along with you', whereas 'push' means 'to move something away from you'.

6) steady
'wobbly' means 'unstable', whereas 'steady' means 'stable'.

7) certain
'unsure' means 'unconvinced', whereas 'certain' means 'convinced'.

8) harm
'aid' means 'to help', whereas 'harm' means 'to hurt'.

9) parent
'child' means 'a son or daughter', whereas 'parent' means 'a mother or father'.

10) shrink
'swell' means 'to get bigger', whereas 'shrink' means 'to get smaller'.

11) bald
'hairy' means 'covered with hair', whereas 'bald' means 'without hair'.

12) fire
'hire' means 'to give someone a job', whereas 'fire' means 'to sack someone from a job'.

13) countryside
'city' means 'an urban area', whereas 'countryside' means 'a rural area'.

14) unfashionable
'trendy' means 'popular', whereas 'unfashionable' means 'unpopular'.

15) prevent
'cause' means 'to make something happen', whereas 'prevent' means 'to stop something happening'.

Section 2: Verbal Reasoning — Synonyms

1) increase
Both words mean 'to make bigger'.

2) regularly
Both words mean 'frequently'.

3) pleasure
Both words mean 'a feeling of happiness'.

4) incorrect
Both words mean 'untrue'.

5) mention
Both words mean 'to express with words'.

6) picture
Both words mean 'a photograph'.

7) border
Both words mean 'a boundary'.

8) scorched
Both words mean 'damaged by fire'.

9) display
Both words mean 'to demonstrate'.

10) award
Both words mean 'something that shows recognition of achievement'.

11) pimple
Both words mean 'a blemish on the skin'.

12) chunk
Both words mean 'a part'.

13) employer
Both words mean 'the person who is in charge of a worker'.

14) ideal
Both words mean 'exactly right'.

15) barrier
Both words mean 'something that separates two areas of land'.

Section 3: Numerical Reasoning

1) Japan, Red, Black, North
Compare the digits in each place, from left to right. Both the Sea of Japan and the Red Sea have 3 in the thousands place. The Sea of Japan has 7 hundreds and the Red Sea has 0 hundreds, so the Sea of Japan has the largest depth. The Black Sea has 2 in the thousands place, and the North Sea doesn't have any thousands (it's only a three-digit number). So the list in order from largest to smallest depth is:
Sea of Japan, Red Sea, Black Sea, North Sea.

2) 80 °C
An anticlockwise turn means the temperature will go down. One quarter of the dial is 3 of the divisions, so the dial ends up on 80 °C.

3) 3680
Hannah's number has 3 in the thousands column and 8 in the tens column, so only 3680 can be the correct option.

4 a) parallelogram
It can't be a square or a rhombus since the sides aren't all the same length. A rectangle only has 90° angles so that can also be ruled out. If the shape was a kite then one of the sides next to the 8 cm side would also be 8 cm, but they both look smaller. So it must be a parallelogram.

4 b) 5 cm
In a parallelogram, opposite sides have the same length. So a = 5 cm.

5) 26
The full number line covers 18 to 38, and 38 − 18 = 20.
There are 10 divisions, so each of these covers 20 ÷ 10 = 2.
The circled number is 4 divisions from 18, so its value is
18 + (4 × 2) = 18 + 8 = 26.

6 a) 9
Each horizontal line represents 4 ÷ 2 = 2 children. The bar for clarinet is halfway between 8 and 10, which is 9 children.

6 b) 15
Find how many children were given an instrument
by reading off the heights of all the bars.
Flute: 12. Violin: 2. Guitar: 20. Piano: 17. Clarinet: 9.
Then add all of these up: 12 + 2 + 20 + 17 + 9 = 60.
So 60 of the 75 children were given an instrument
and 75 − 60 = 15 were not.

7) 22
Only the cube faces on the outside of the shape will be painted.
There are 6 faces on the front of the shape, 6 faces on the back,
3 faces on the bottom, 3 faces on the top and 2 faces
on each side. So 6 + 6 + 3 + 3 + 2 + 2 = 22 faces will be painted.

8) 980 miles
You can use the column method for addition:
```
   7 6 6
 + 2 1 5
   ─────
   9 8 1
       1
```
You're rounding the 8 in the tens column, so look at the digit to the right of it (in the ones column). It's a 1, so round down to 980 miles.

9 a) 5
Reading from the last column in the table, Henry VIII had 6 wives and Charles II had 1 wife. So Charles II had 6 − 1 = 5 fewer wives than Henry VIII.

9 b) 1087
Reading from the first column, William I had his coronation in 1066. Use partitioning to do 1066 + 21: 1066 + 20 = 1086 and 1086 + 1 = 1087, so 1066 + 21 = 1087.

9 c) 44
Count on from 1559 to 1603 to find the answer:
Add 1 to get to 1560, then 40 to get to 1600 and another 3 to get to 1603. So there were 1 + 40 + 3 = 44 years between Elizabeth I's coronation and death.

10 a) 70
If there are 5 trophies on 7 shelves then that means there are 7 × 5 = 35 trophies in total. Each of these has 2 handles, so that's 2 × 35 = 70 handles.

10 b) 14
You know from part a) that there are 35 trophies in the cabinet.
$\frac{1}{5}$ of 35 = 35 ÷ 5 = 7, so $\frac{2}{5}$ of 35 = 7 × 2 = 14.

11) D
A and B have no lines of symmetry. C is a regular hexagon with 6 lines of symmetry and E is a square so it has 4 lines of symmetry. The three lines of symmetry of shape D are:

12) 0
If you multiply any number by 0, the answer is always 0.

13) 55 g
550 g is about the weight of a pack of margarine, so 550 g, 5.5 kg and 55 kg are too heavy for a hen's egg. A teaspoon of water weighs about 5 g, so 5.5 g is too light for a hen's egg. So 55 g is the best estimate for the weight of a hen's egg.

14 a) 6
Elijah saw ◯ × 2 = 4 × 2 = 8 bubbles. Jackie's row in the pictogram contains a ◖ symbol, which is half of ◯, so it stands for 4 ÷ 2 = 2 bubbles.
So Jackie saw ◯ × 3 + ◖ = 4 × 3 + 2 = 12 + 2 = 14 bubbles.
That means Elijah saw 14 − 8 = 6 fewer bubbles.

14 b) 54
You know from part a) that Elijah saw 8 bubbles and Jackie saw 14 bubbles. Selwyn saw ◯ × 3 = 4 × 3 = 12 bubbles and Varesh saw ◯ × 5 = 4 × 5 = 20 bubbles. The total number of bubbles seen was 8 + 14 + 12 + 20 = 54 bubbles.

14 c) $\frac{12}{54}$
From part b), you know that Selwyn saw 12 bubbles and the total number of bubbles seen was 54. So, as a fraction, Selwyn saw $\frac{12}{54}$ of the bubbles.

15 a) B
The sides of this octagon all have the same length, so it goes in either sections A or B. Looking at the angles, they're all greater than 90° so the shape has no acute angles. This means it goes in section B.

15 b) C
A scalene triangle has sides that aren't the same length, so it's going to have to go in sections C or D. No matter how you draw a scalene triangle (see some examples below), at least two of the angles must be less than 90°. So it goes in section C.

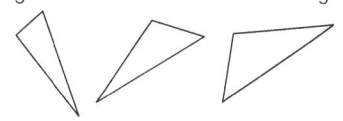

16) 8
The difference between 9.5 and 6.5 is 3. So the number that is halfway between the two of them must be 3 ÷ 2 = 1.5 away from them both. So the answer is 6.5 + 1.5 = 8. You can check by adding on 1.5 again: 8 + 1.5 = 9.5, as you'd expect.

17 a) 25 days
There are 7 days in a week, so there are 3 × 7 = 21 days in 3 weeks. Add on the additional 4 days to get 21 + 4 = 25 days.

17 b) Friday
The number of weeks isn't important (you can add on as many weeks as you like and you'll just keep coming back around to Monday), so just concentrate on the additional number of days. Count on 4 days after Monday: Tuesday, Wednesday, Thursday, Friday.

18 a) 6
For each of the three meals there are two different drinks options — orange juice or mineral water. So there are 3 × 2 = 6 different combinations of a meal and a drink.

18 b) £12.65
Work out how much Monica needs to pay: £6.40 + 95p.
95p = £1 − 5p, so first add on £1 to £6.40: £6.40 + £1 = £7.40.
Then subtract 5p: £7.40 − 5p = £7.40 − £0.05 = £7.35.
Subtract this from £20 to work out how much change Monica got: £7 less than £20 is £13 and 35p less than £13 is £12.65.

19) 5400
9 × 6 = 54 and 600 = 6 × 100.
So, 9 × 600 = 54 × 100 = 5400.

20 a) 4 squares left, 3 squares down
Pick a point on A and match it to the corresponding point on B, counting how many squares you move in each direction. E.g. using the point in the bottom-left corner of the shapes:

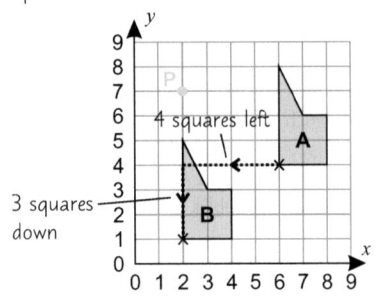

20 b) (5, 6)
Slide P three squares to the right and one square down and see where it ends up:

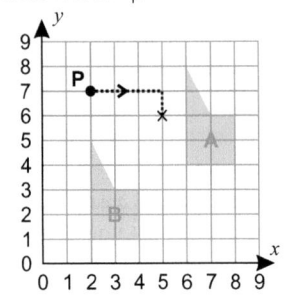

21 a) 1.74 kg
To divide by 100, move all the digits two places to the right. So 174 kg ÷ 100 = 1.74 kg.

21 b) 859 kg
Use column subtraction to find the difference between the weights:

$$\begin{array}{r} \cancel{1}^{9}\cancel{0}^{12}\cancel{3}^{1}3 \\ -\ \ 1\ 7\ 4 \\ \hline 8\ 5\ 9 \end{array}$$

22) 49
X = 10, L = 50 and I = 1.
X appears before the larger L, so XL = 50 − 10 = 40.
I appears before the larger X, so IX = 10 − 1 = 9.
So the number is 40 + 9 = 49.

23 a) 303 mm
Change the units so both lengths are in the same units — mm are easier to use here. 1 cm = 10 mm, so 36 cm = 360 mm. So the difference between their hair lengths is 360 − 57 = 303 mm.

23 b) 6 cm
10 mm = 1 cm, so 57 mm = 57 ÷ 10 = 5.7 cm. To round to the nearest centimetre, look at the digit in the tenths column. It's 7, so round up to give 6 cm.

24 a) 72
4 + 5 = 9, 9 × 8 = 72.

24 b) 6
Work backwards through the machine:
88 ÷ 8 = 11, 11 − 5 = 6
(To make sure you've got the answer right, you can put 6 into the machine and check that you get 88 out of it.)

25) 1/2
5/12 + 1/12 = 6/12 = 1/2 of his games are either action or puzzle.
So 1 − 1/2 = 1/2 are not action or puzzle.

26 a) 35
Read off how many carrots the greengrocer had at 10 am (= 10:00) and at 1 pm (= 13:00). At 10 am, the greengrocer had 50 carrots. At 1 pm, the greengrocer had 15 carrots. So she sold 50 − 15 = 35 carrots between these two times.

26 b) 15:00 - 16:00
If the greengrocer had a delivery of carrots then you'd expect to see an increase in the number of carrots that she has in stock. This happens between 15:00 and 16:00.

27 a) 616
Multiply the number of desks by the number of chairs.
You can use short multiplication:

$$\begin{array}{r} 1\ 5\ 4 \\ \times\ \ \ \ \ 4 \\ \hline 6\ 1\ 6 \\ {\scriptstyle 2\ 1} \end{array}$$

27 b) 77
Partition 154 into 150 and 4, and divide each part by 2 separately:
150 ÷ 2 = 75 and 4 ÷ 2 = 2, so half of 154 = 75 + 2 = 77.

27 c) 11
You need to work out how many 14s go into 154:
140 ÷ 14 = 10 and 140 + 14 = 154, so 154 ÷ 14 = 11.

28 a) 125 ml
To make 8 glasses of fruit drink you need 250 ml of lemon juice. To make 4 glasses of fruit drink, you'd need 250 ÷ 2 = 125 ml of lemon juice.

28 b) 3
1 lime makes 8 glasses, so 2 limes make 16 glasses and 3 limes make 24 glasses. 2 whole limes isn't enough, so you'll need 3.

28 c) 1500 ml
1 litre = 1000 ml, which is needed to make 8 glasses of fruit drink. So 1000 ml ÷ 2 = 500 ml is needed to make 4 glasses. So, to make 12 glasses, you'd need 1000 ml + 500 ml = 1500 ml.

29) 9
The UK takes up a quarter of the circle, so a quarter of the people answered that they'd rather go on holiday in the UK.
1/4 of 36 = 36 ÷ 4 = 9.

30 a) £18.00
The 4-pack works out as £2.40 ÷ 4 = £0.60 per roll.
The 9-pack works out as £4.50 ÷ 9 = £0.50 per roll.
The 12-pack works out as £9.60 ÷ 12 = £0.80 per roll.
So the 9-pack is the cheapest option of the three.
36 ÷ 9 = 4, so you'll need to buy 4 of these to have 36 rolls, which will cost: £4.50 × 4 = £18.

30 b) £3.00
1/3 of £4.50 = £4.50 ÷ 3 = £1.50.
So 2/3 of £4.50 = 2 × £1.50 = £3.

CGP

11+ Practice Papers

For the **CEM** test

Answer Sheets

Ages 8-9

BLANK PAGE

Using the Multiple Choice Answer Sheets

If you're doing a Multiple Choice paper, it's often marked by a computer. These papers use special answer sheets like the ones in this booklet.

There's a Multiple Choice answer sheet to go with each Practice Paper, so make sure you're filling in the right one. If you get used to these answer sheets now, it means there'll be no nasty surprises when you sit the real test.

Here are a few tips for using the answer sheets without getting yourself in a pickle...

Tips for Filling in the Answer Sheets

1) Before you start, fill in your name and the name of your school in the correct space. There may be boxes for other information, like your date of birth or your pupil number. Make sure you don't leave anything blank by mistake.

2) To mark your answer, put a clear pencil line through the answer box.

3) Make sure you have a pencil sharpener and an eraser for any mistakes.

4) If you make a mistake, rub out the incorrect answer first, and then fill in your new answer clearly.

5) It's easy to lose your place when you move from the practice paper to the answer sheet, so match up the question number on the paper and the answer sheet. Keeping the two sheets close together will help you do this.

6) If you skip a question to come back to later, make sure you leave a gap for that question on the answer sheet. That way your answers will stay in order.

7) Don't do rough working on your answer sheet.

8) Don't worry if you mark boxes in the same position several times in a row — just because you've marked the second box four times, it doesn't mean that your answers are wrong.

Set A: Paper 1

Pupil's name:

School name:

Test date:

Pupil Number

School Number

Date of Birth

Please mark like this: ▬

Set A: Paper 1

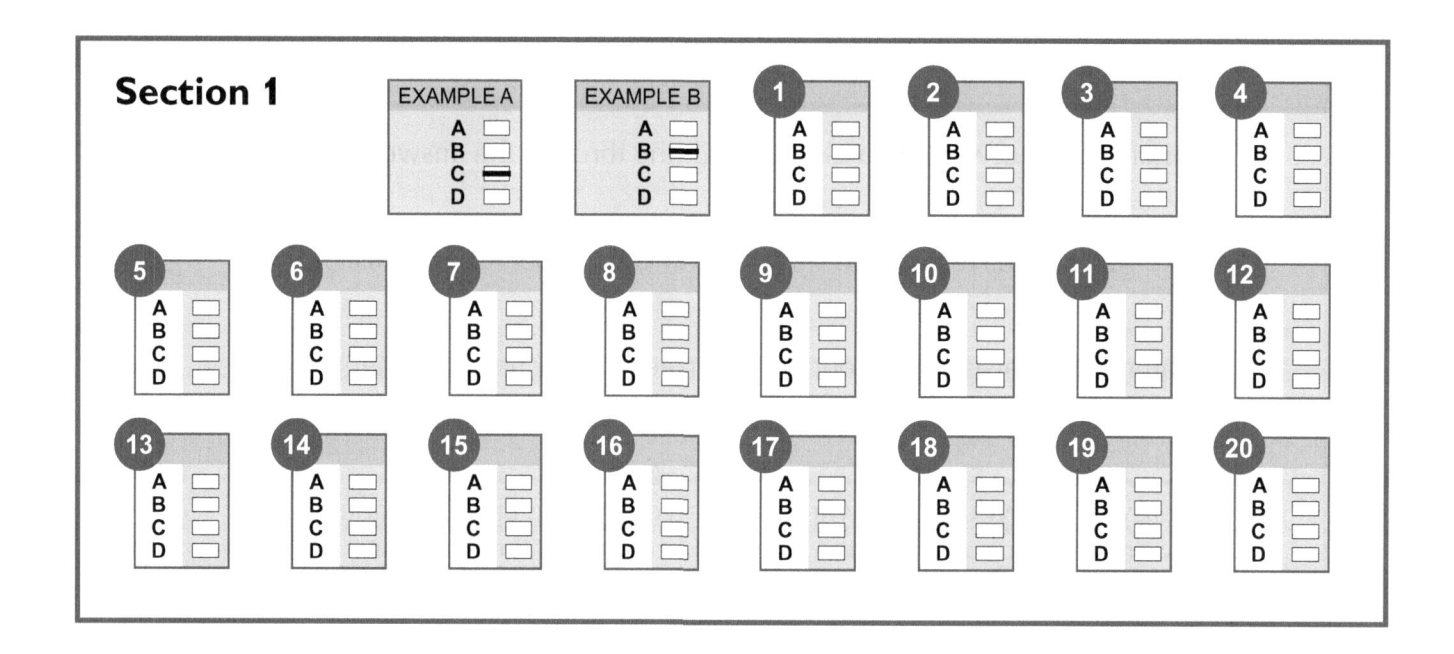

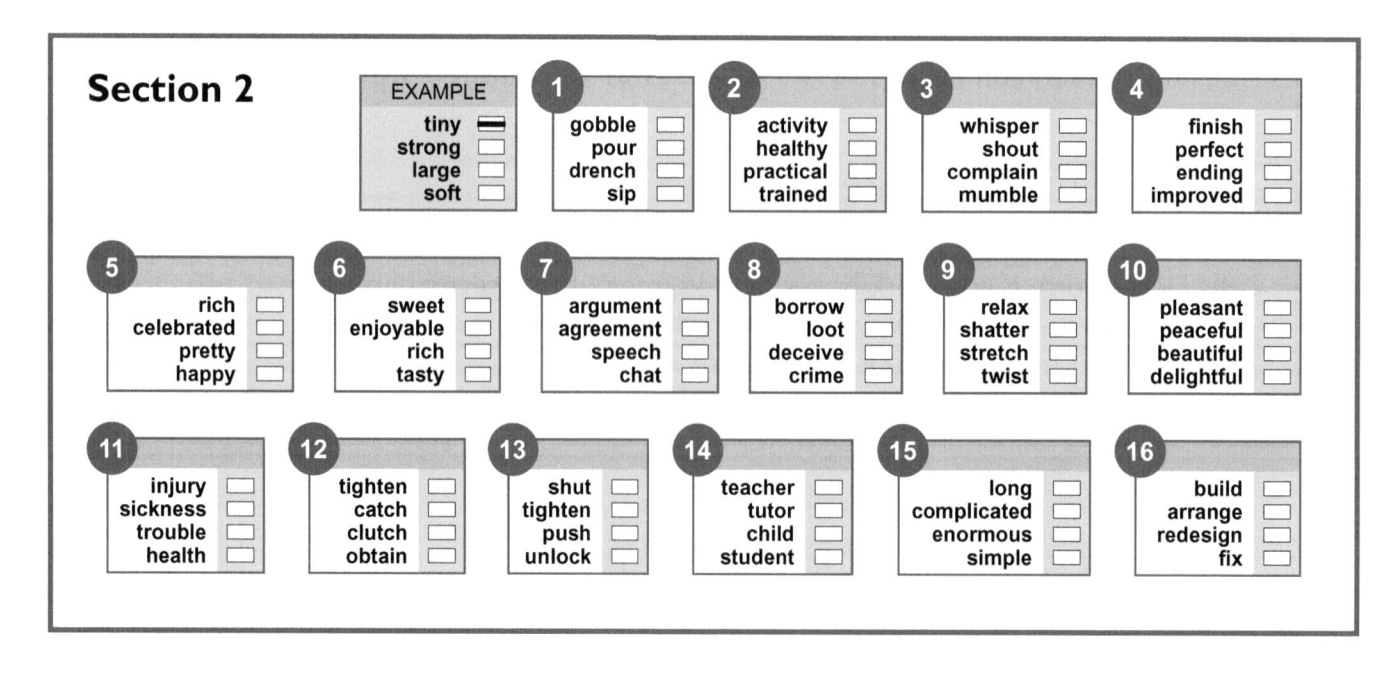

Section 1

EXAMPLE A, EXAMPLE B, 1–20 (options A, B, C, D for each)

Section 2

EXAMPLE: tiny, strong, large, soft

1. gobble, pour, drench, sip
2. activity, healthy, practical, trained
3. whisper, shout, complain, mumble
4. finish, perfect, ending, improved
5. rich, celebrated, pretty, happy
6. sweet, enjoyable, rich, tasty
7. argument, agreement, speech, chat
8. borrow, loot, deceive, crime
9. relax, shatter, stretch, twist
10. pleasant, peaceful, beautiful, delightful
11. injury, sickness, trouble, health
12. tighten, catch, clutch, obtain
13. shut, tighten, push, unlock
14. teacher, tutor, child, student
15. long, complicated, enormous, simple
16. build, arrange, redesign, fix

11+ / CEM / 8-9 / Answer Sheets — © CGP 2019

Section 3

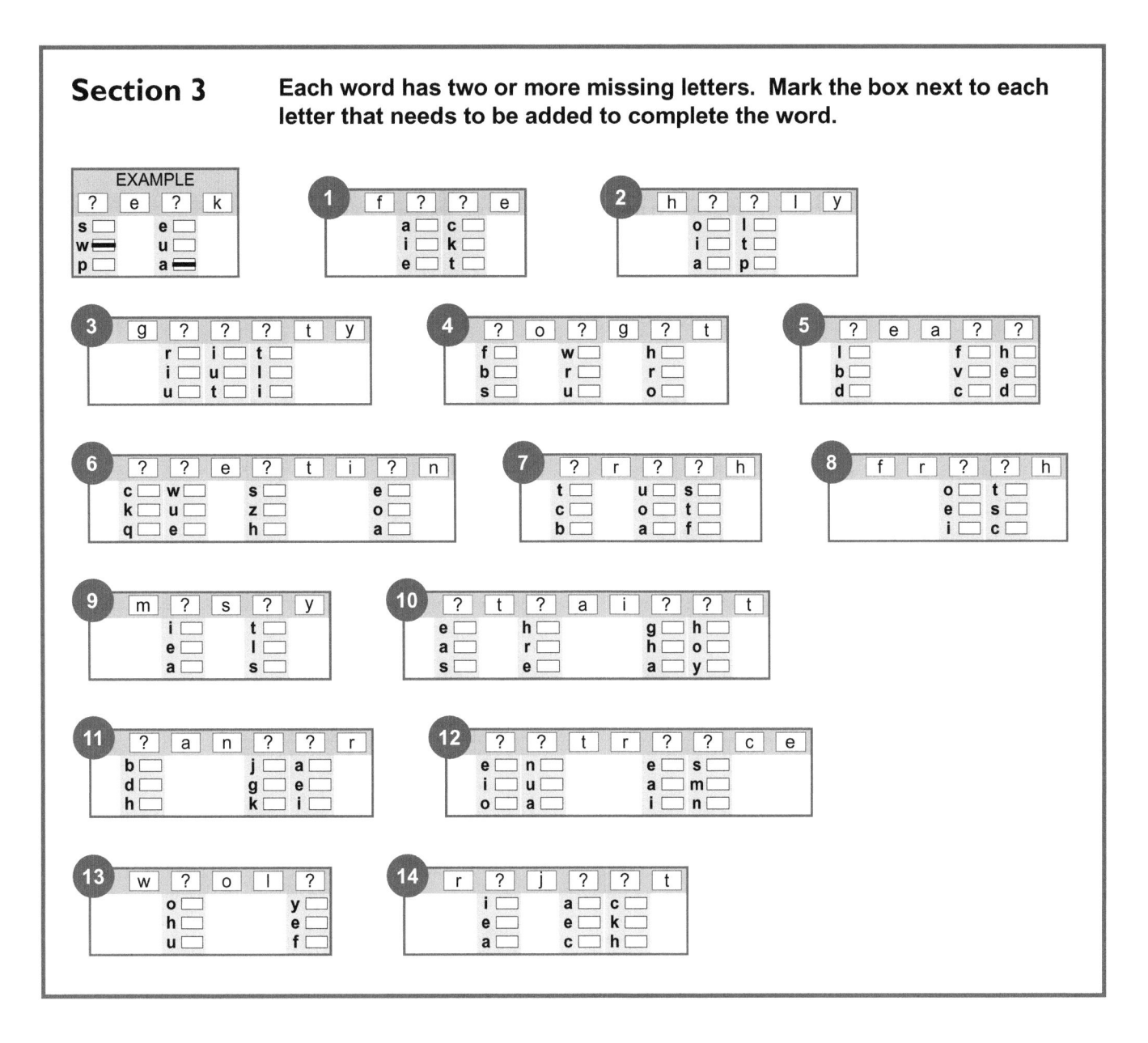

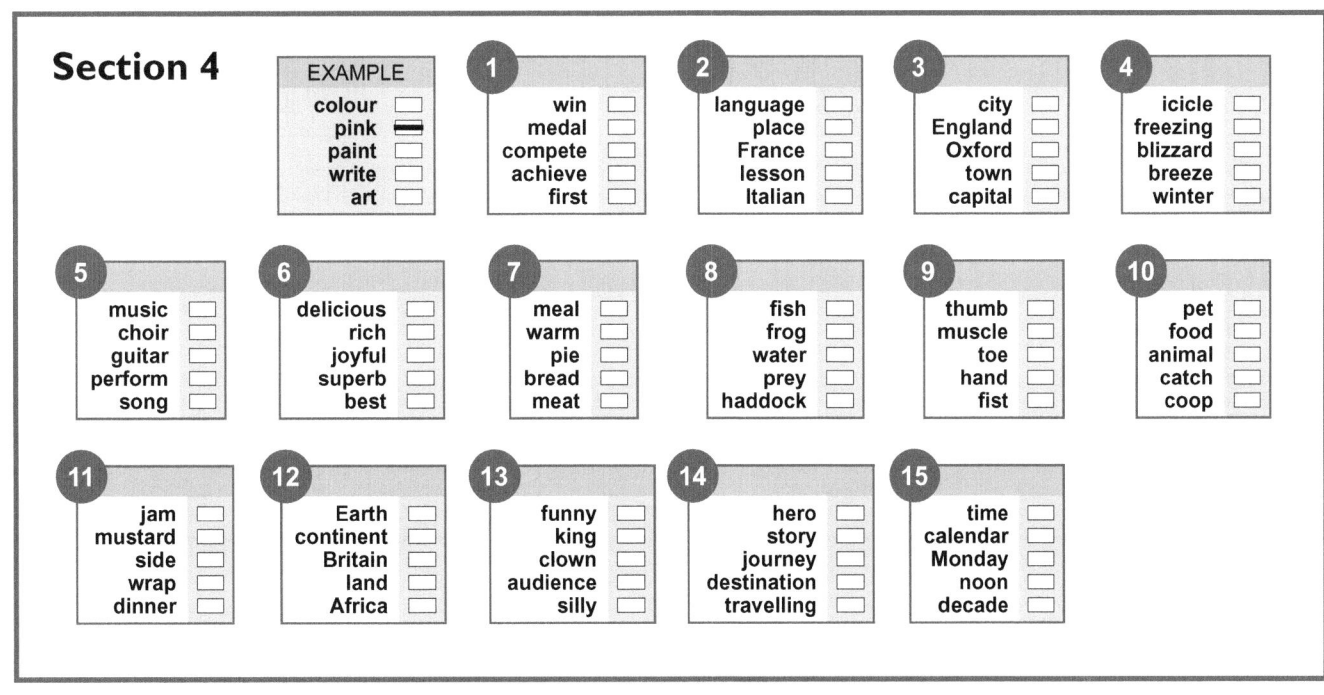

Each word has two or more missing letters. Mark the box next to each letter that needs to be added to complete the word.

EXAMPLE: ? e ? k — w, a (week/weak... wa → weak)

1. f ? ? e — options: a/c, i/k, e/t
2. h ? ? l y — options: o/l, i/t, a/p
3. g ? ? ? t y — options: r/i/t, i/u/l, u/t/i
4. ? o ? g ? t — options: f/w/h, b/r/r, s/u/o
5. ? e a ? ? — options: l/f/h, b/v/e, d/c/d
6. ? ? e ? t i ? n — options: c/w/s/e, k/u/z/o, q/e/h/a
7. ? r ? h — options: t/u/s, c/o/t, b/a/f
8. f r ? ? h — options: o/t, e/s, i/c
9. m ? s ? y — options: i/t, e/l, a/s
10. ? t ? a i ? ? t — options: e/h/g/h, a/r/h/o, s/e/a/y
11. ? a n ? ? r — options: b/j/a, d/g/e, h/k/i
12. ? ? t r ? ? c e — options: e/n/e/s, i/u/a/m, o/a/i/n
13. w ? o l ? — options: o/y, h/e, u/f
14. r ? j ? ? t — options: i/a/c, e/e/k, a/c/h

Section 4

EXAMPLE: colour, **pink**, paint, write, art

1. win, medal, compete, achieve, first
2. language, place, France, lesson, Italian
3. city, England, Oxford, town, capital
4. icicle, freezing, blizzard, breeze, winter
5. music, choir, guitar, perform, song
6. delicious, rich, joyful, superb, best
7. meal, warm, pie, bread, meat
8. fish, frog, water, prey, haddock
9. thumb, muscle, toe, hand, fist
10. pet, food, animal, catch, coop
11. jam, mustard, side, wrap, dinner
12. Earth, continent, Britain, land, Africa
13. funny, king, clown, audience, silly
14. hero, story, journey, destination, travelling
15. time, calendar, Monday, noon, decade

Section 5

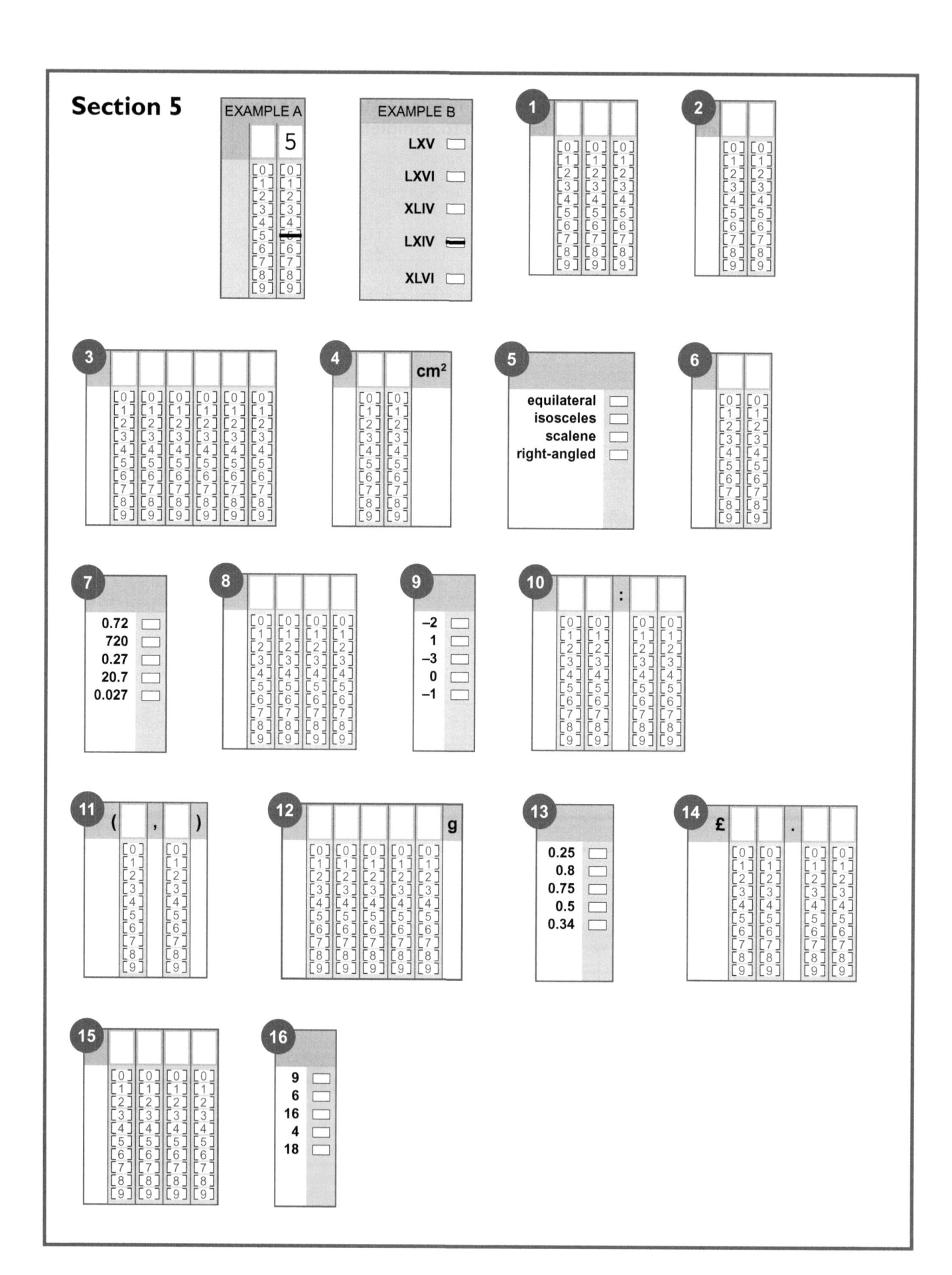

Section 6

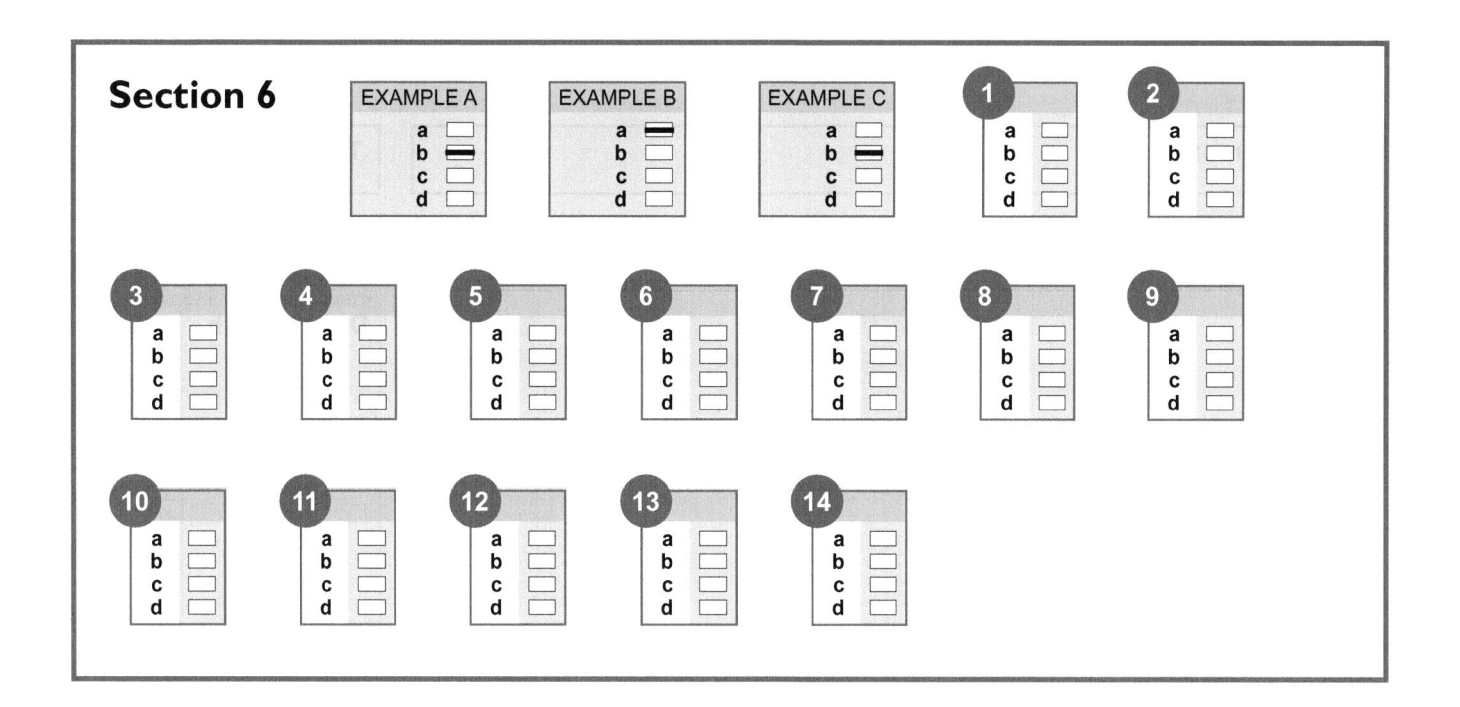

EXAMPLE A	EXAMPLE B	EXAMPLE C
a ☐	a ■	a ☐
b ■	b ☐	b ■
c ☐	c ☐	c ☐
d ☐	d ☐	d ☐

1. a ☐ b ☐ c ☐ d ☐
2. a ☐ b ☐ c ☐ d ☐
3. a ☐ b ☐ c ☐ d ☐
4. a ☐ b ☐ c ☐ d ☐
5. a ☐ b ☐ c ☐ d ☐
6. a ☐ b ☐ c ☐ d ☐
7. a ☐ b ☐ c ☐ d ☐
8. a ☐ b ☐ c ☐ d ☐
9. a ☐ b ☐ c ☐ d ☐
10. a ☐ b ☐ c ☐ d ☐
11. a ☐ b ☐ c ☐ d ☐
12. a ☐ b ☐ c ☐ d ☐
13. a ☐ b ☐ c ☐ d ☐
14. a ☐ b ☐ c ☐ d ☐

Set A: Paper 2

Pupil's name:

School name:

Test date:

Please mark like this: ▬

Set A: Paper 2

Pupil Number | School Number | Date of Birth (Day / Month / Year)

Section 1

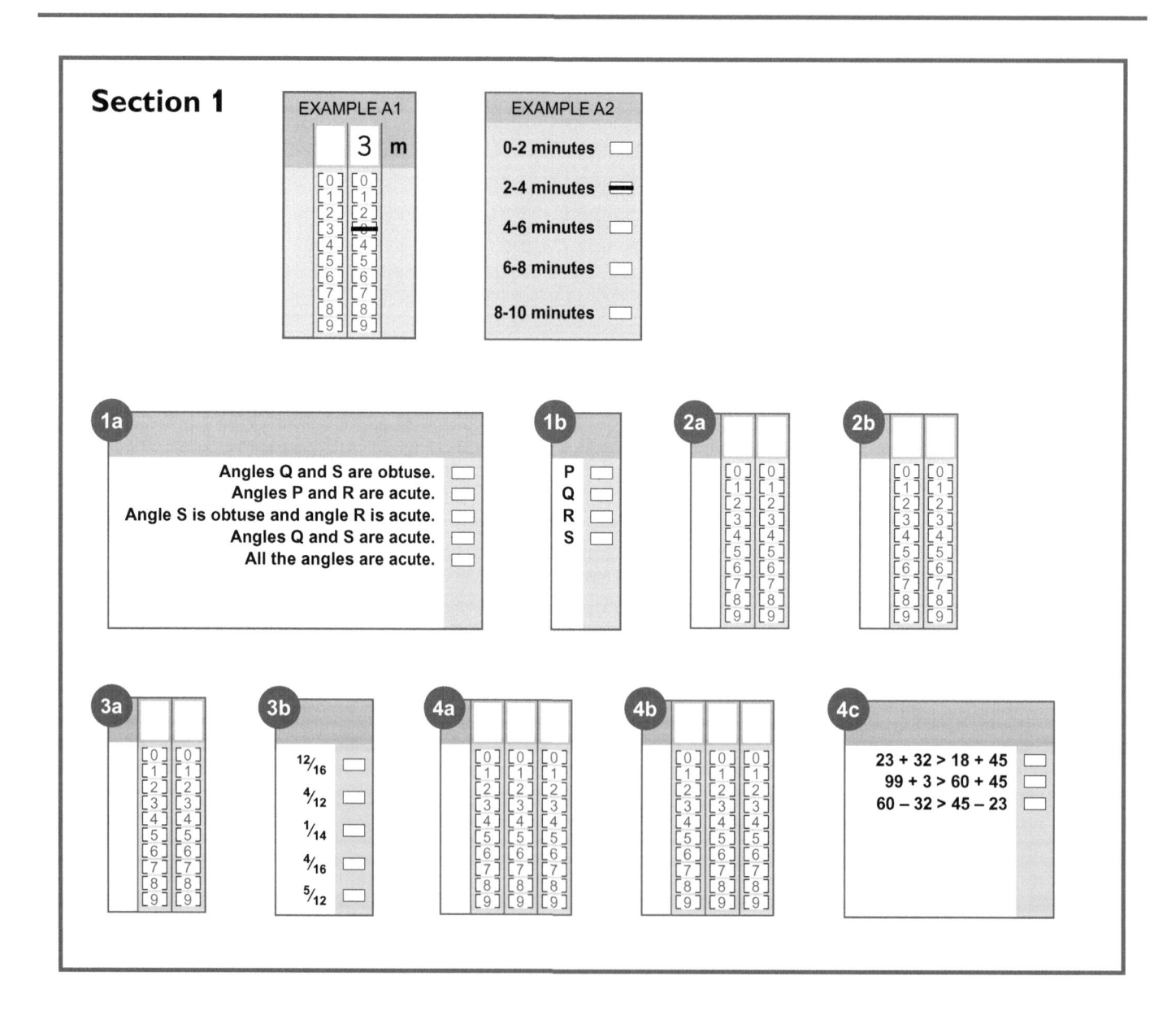

EXAMPLE A1: 3 m

EXAMPLE A2:
- 0-2 minutes
- 2-4 minutes ▬
- 4-6 minutes
- 6-8 minutes
- 8-10 minutes

1a
- Angles Q and S are obtuse.
- Angles P and R are acute.
- Angle S is obtuse and angle R is acute.
- Angles Q and S are acute.
- All the angles are acute.

1b
- P
- Q
- R
- S

2a

2b

3a

3b
- 12/16
- 4/12
- 1/14
- 4/16
- 5/12

4a

4b

4c
- 23 + 32 > 18 + 45
- 99 + 3 > 60 + 45
- 60 − 32 > 45 − 23

11+ / CEM / 8-9 / Answer Sheets
© CGP 2019

Section 1 Continued

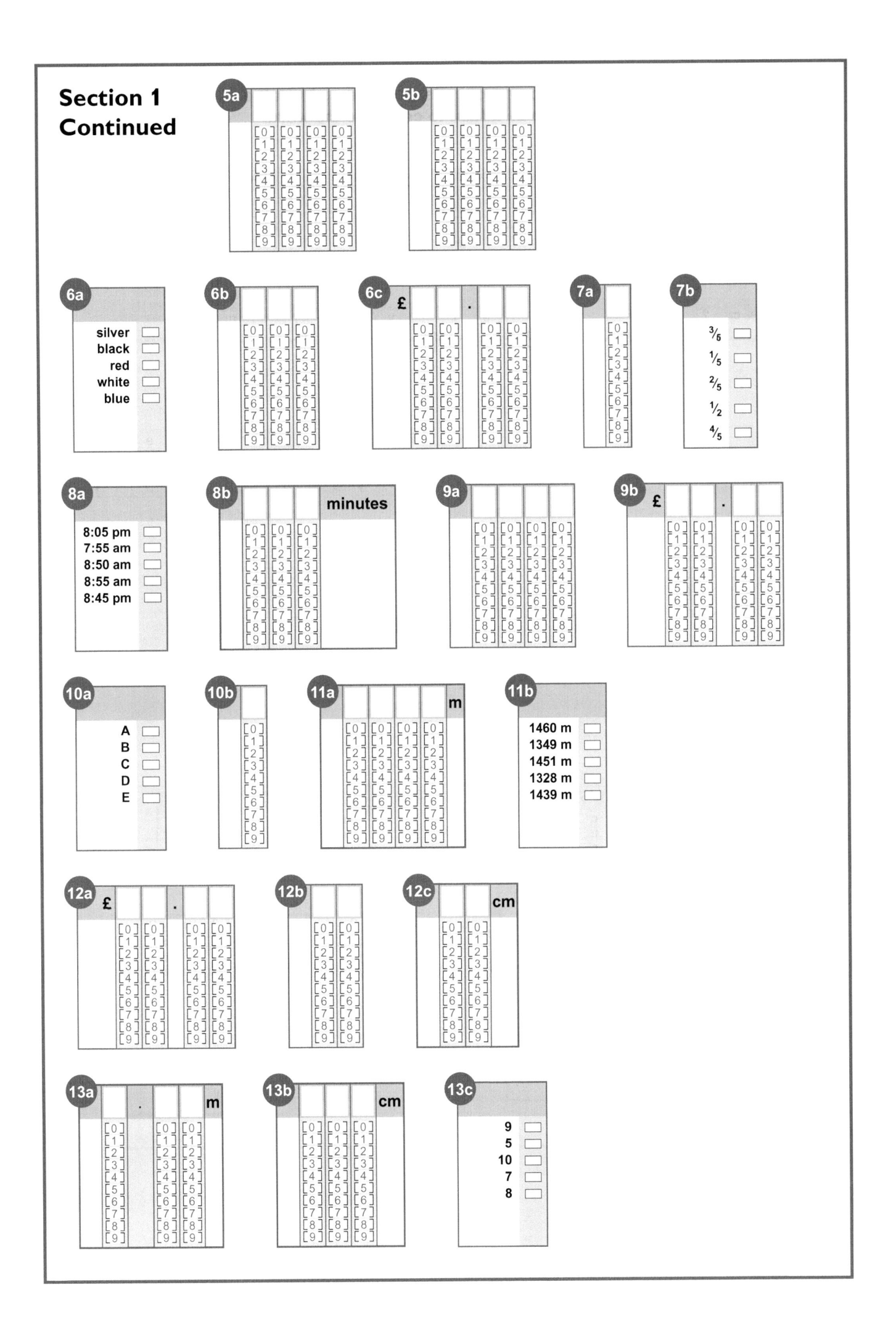

5a
[0] [1] [2] [3] [4] [5] [6] [7] [8] [9] (×4)

5b
[0] [1] [2] [3] [4] [5] [6] [7] [8] [9] (×4)

6a
silver ☐
black ☐
red ☐
white ☐
blue ☐

6b
[0] [1] [2] [3] [4] [5] [6] [7] [8] [9] (×3)

6c £ _ _ . _ _

7a
[0] [1] [2] [3] [4] [5] [6] [7] [8] [9]

7b
$^{3}/_{5}$ ☐
$^{1}/_{5}$ ☐
$^{2}/_{5}$ ☐
$^{1}/_{2}$ ☐
$^{4}/_{5}$ ☐

8a
8:05 pm ☐
7:55 am ☐
8:50 am ☐
8:55 am ☐
8:45 pm ☐

8b _ _ _ minutes

9a
[0] [1] [2] [3] [4] [5] [6] [7] [8] [9] (×4)

9b £ _ _ . _ _

10a
A ☐
B ☐
C ☐
D ☐
E ☐

10b
[0] [1] [2] [3] [4] [5] [6] [7] [8] [9]

11a _ _ _ _ m

11b
1460 m ☐
1349 m ☐
1451 m ☐
1328 m ☐
1439 m ☐

12a £ _ _ . _ _

12b
[0] [1] [2] [3] [4] [5] [6] [7] [8] [9] (×2)

12c _ _ cm

13a _ . _ _ m

13b _ _ _ cm

13c
9 ☐
5 ☐
10 ☐
7 ☐
8 ☐

Section 2

Each word has two or more missing letters. Mark the box next to each letter that needs to be added to complete the word.

EXAMPLE A: p ? ? n ? t s — l, a, e (planets)

EXAMPLE B: ? h ? r d — t, i (third)

EXAMPLE C: V ? ? ? s — e, n, u (Venus)

1. o c ? ? r — options: c, k, q / a, o, u
2. ? e l ? v i ? ? o n — options: h, r, t / e, i, y / r, s, z / h, i, u
3. m ? ? o r — options: a, e, i / g, j, n
4. ? i s t ? r ? — options: h, r, s / e, o, u / e, i, y
5. r e ? e n ? — options: c, s, t / r, s, t
6. s ? l ? ? e r s — options: e, o, u / d, g, j / d, i, r
7. r e ? o v ? r — options: c, k, l / a, e, i
8. p o ? ? l ? r — options: m, p, t / p, o, u / a, e, o
9. i ? v ? l ? e d — options: n, m, p / e, o, u / h, r, v
10. w ? ? e l c ? a i ? s — options: h, e, i / e, i, y / c, h, s / r, s, t
11. ? e c ? m e — options: b, d, f / a, e, y
12. e x ? a n ? ? d — options: p, r, t / d, l, s / a, e, i
13. r a ? ? e — options: i, n, m / g, j, y
14. ? r ? w n — options: b, g, t / a, o, u
15. ? m ? o r t ? n t — options: e, i, o / p, r, t / a, e, i
16. c o ? ? i n ? e — options: n, m, p / r, t, s / u, w, y

Section 3

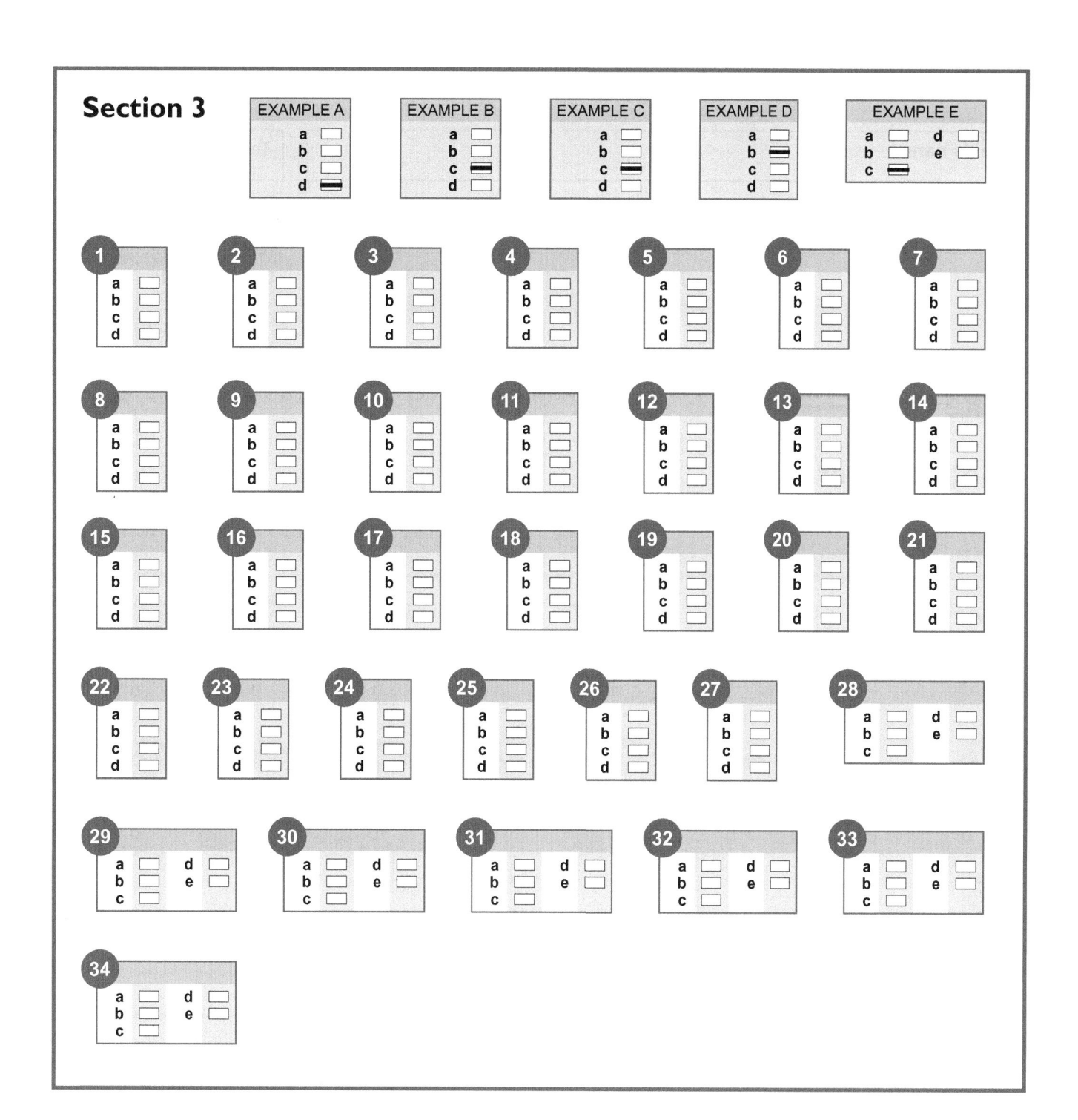

EXAMPLE A: d
EXAMPLE B: c
EXAMPLE C: c
EXAMPLE D: b
EXAMPLE E: c

Questions 1–27: options a, b, c, d

Questions 28–34: options a, b, c, d, e

Set B: Paper 1

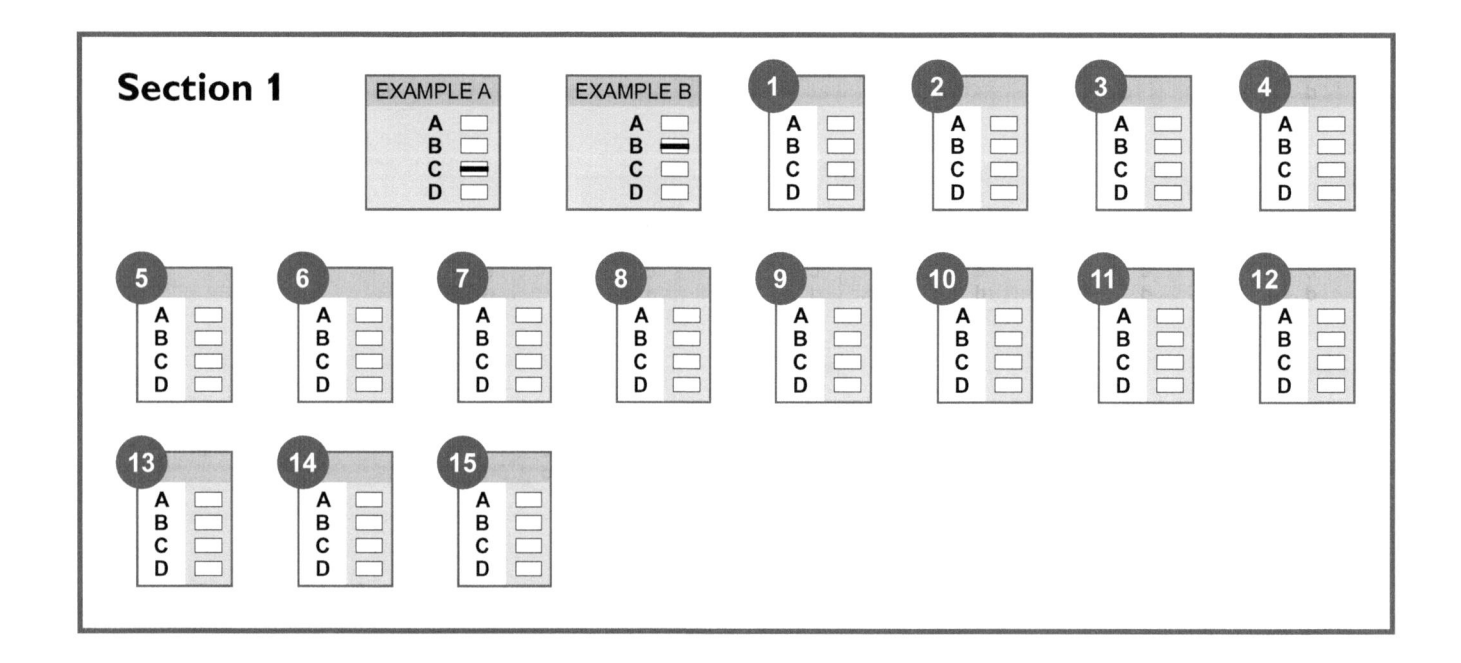

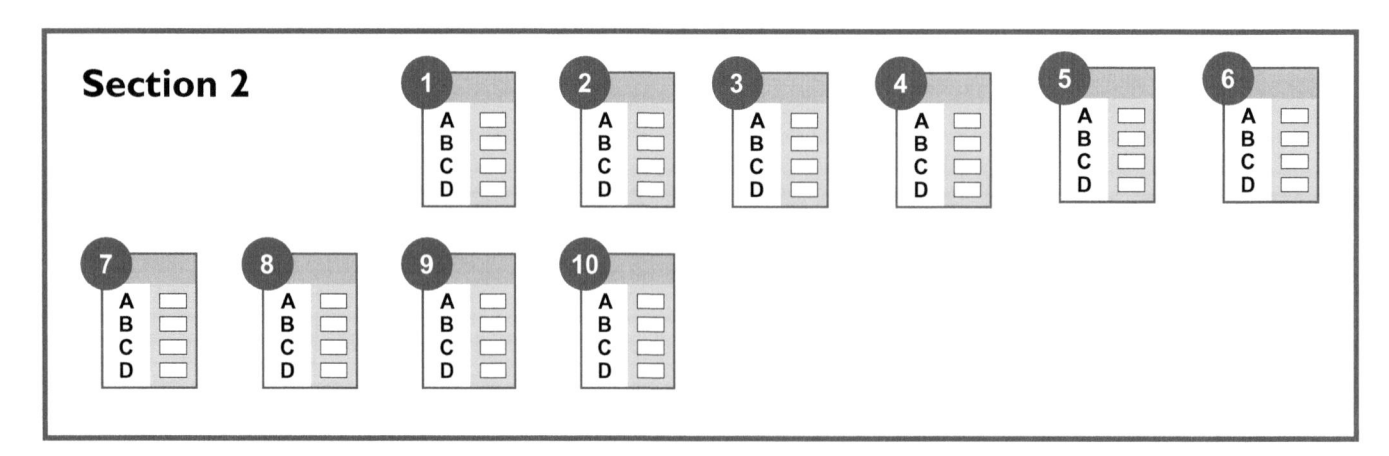

Pupil's name:

School name:

Test date:

Please mark like this: ⊟

Set B: Paper 1

Section 1

Section 2

Section 3

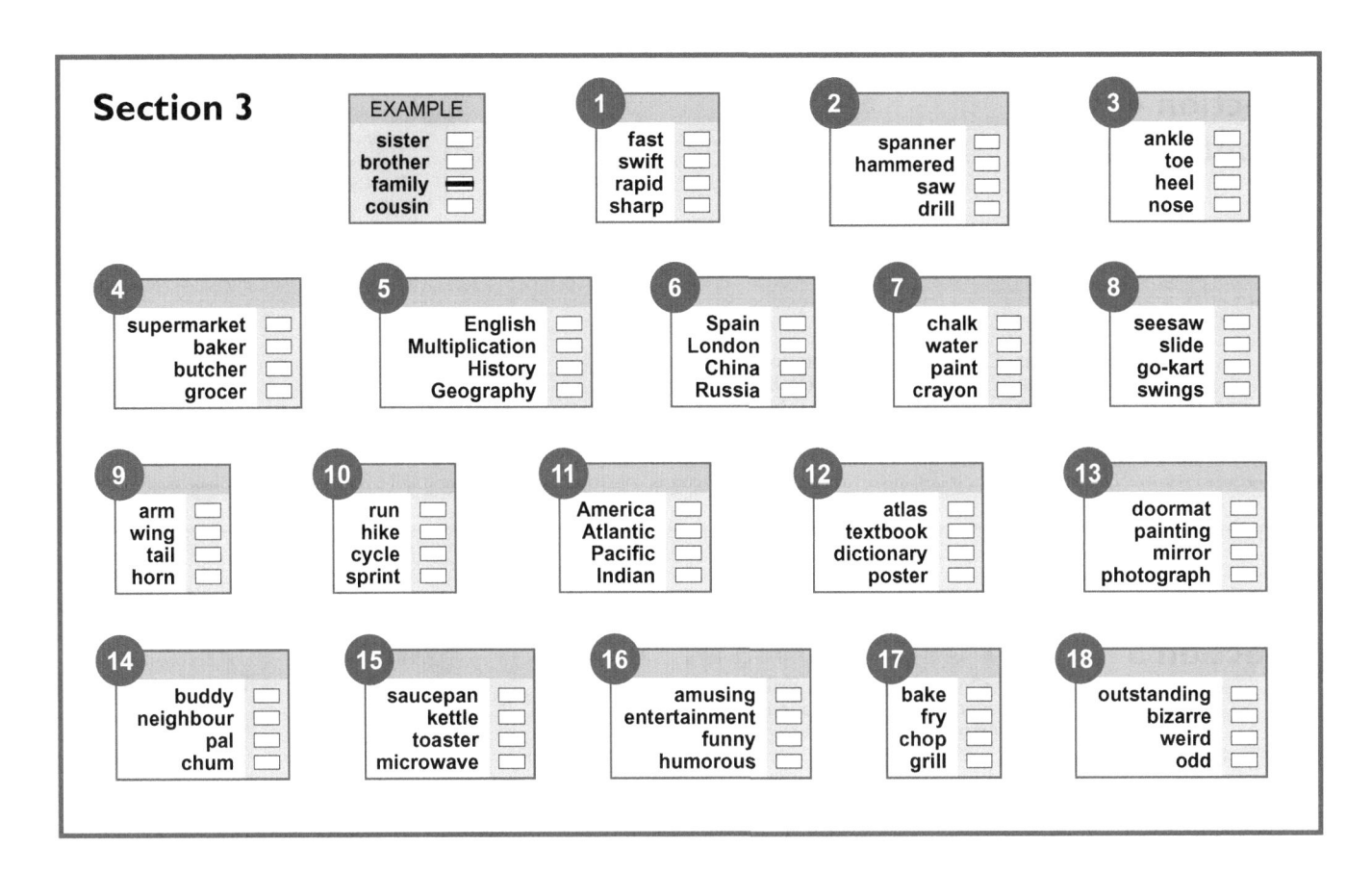

EXAMPLE
- sister ☐
- brother ☐
- family ■
- cousin ☐

1
- fast ☐
- swift ☐
- rapid ☐
- sharp ☐

2
- spanner ☐
- hammered ☐
- saw ☐
- drill ☐

3
- ankle ☐
- toe ☐
- heel ☐
- nose ☐

4
- supermarket ☐
- baker ☐
- butcher ☐
- grocer ☐

5
- English ☐
- Multiplication ☐
- History ☐
- Geography ☐

6
- Spain ☐
- London ☐
- China ☐
- Russia ☐

7
- chalk ☐
- water ☐
- paint ☐
- crayon ☐

8
- seesaw ☐
- slide ☐
- go-kart ☐
- swings ☐

9
- arm ☐
- wing ☐
- tail ☐
- horn ☐

10
- run ☐
- hike ☐
- cycle ☐
- sprint ☐

11
- America ☐
- Atlantic ☐
- Pacific ☐
- Indian ☐

12
- atlas ☐
- textbook ☐
- dictionary ☐
- poster ☐

13
- doormat ☐
- painting ☐
- mirror ☐
- photograph ☐

14
- buddy ☐
- neighbour ☐
- pal ☐
- chum ☐

15
- saucepan ☐
- kettle ☐
- toaster ☐
- microwave ☐

16
- amusing ☐
- entertainment ☐
- funny ☐
- humorous ☐

17
- bake ☐
- fry ☐
- chop ☐
- grill ☐

18
- outstanding ☐
- bizarre ☐
- weird ☐
- odd ☐

Section 4

EXAMPLE
- it ☐
- for ☐
- time ☐
- was ☐
- late ■
- bed ☐

1
- she ☐
- down ☐
- waiting ☐
- the ☐
- long ☐
- sprinted ☐
- path ☐

2
- remember ☐
- actor ☐
- performed ☐
- couldn't ☐
- the ☐
- lines ☐
- his ☐

3
- mansion ☐
- is ☐
- by ☐
- haunted ☐
- ghosts ☐
- the ☐
- terrify ☐

4
- not ☐
- poisonous ☐
- snakes ☐
- threat ☐
- all ☐
- are ☐

5
- to ☐
- Satoshi ☐
- cards ☐
- played ☐
- trading ☐
- loved ☐
- collect ☐

6
- on ☐
- hated ☐
- Joel ☐
- pizza ☐
- like ☐
- mushrooms ☐
- his ☐

7
- are ☐
- sugary ☐
- for ☐
- taste ☐
- your ☐
- bad ☐
- sweets ☐
- teeth ☐

8
- stuck ☐
- the ☐
- was ☐
- on ☐
- finish ☐
- Millie ☐
- puzzle ☐
- final ☐

9
- he ☐
- tyre ☐
- car ☐
- very ☐
- the ☐
- drove ☐
- slowly ☐

10
- looked ☐
- the ☐
- very ☐
- fought ☐
- similar ☐
- brothers ☐

11
- hole ☐
- in ☐
- stripes ☐
- has ☐
- it ☐
- sock ☐
- my ☐
- a ☐

Section 4 Continued

12 people ☐ nervous ☐
speaking ☐
made ☐
public ☐
her ☐

13 over ☐ friend ☐
is ☐ sleeping ☐
best ☐ bed ☐
tonight ☐
my ☐

14 told ☐ dinner ☐
jokes ☐ cackle ☐
hilarious ☐ Zara ☐
many ☐
at ☐

15 started ☐ miss ☐
family ☐ to ☐
his ☐
Nathan ☐
visited ☐

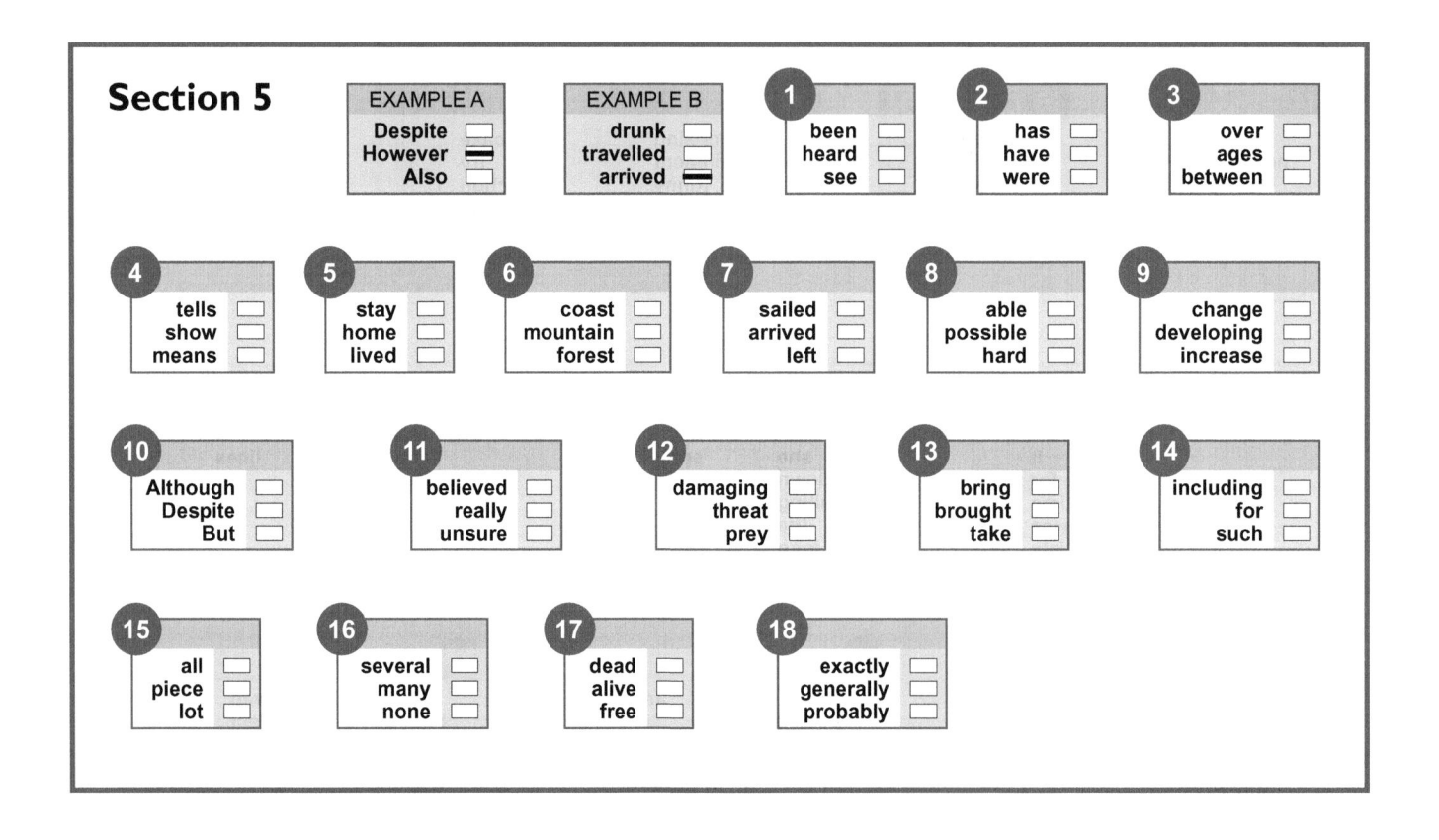

Section 5

EXAMPLE A
Despite ☐
However ■
Also ☐

EXAMPLE B
drunk ☐
travelled ☐
arrived ■

1 been ☐
heard ☐
see ☐

2 has ☐
have ☐
were ☐

3 over ☐
ages ☐
between ☐

4 tells ☐
show ☐
means ☐

5 stay ☐
home ☐
lived ☐

6 coast ☐
mountain ☐
forest ☐

7 sailed ☐
arrived ☐
left ☐

8 able ☐
possible ☐
hard ☐

9 change ☐
developing ☐
increase ☐

10 Although ☐
Despite ☐
But ☐

11 believed ☐
really ☐
unsure ☐

12 damaging ☐
threat ☐
prey ☐

13 bring ☐
brought ☐
take ☐

14 including ☐
for ☐
such ☐

15 all ☐
piece ☐
lot ☐

16 several ☐
many ☐
none ☐

17 dead ☐
alive ☐
free ☐

18 exactly ☐
generally ☐
probably ☐

11+ / CEM / 8-9 / Answer Sheets © CGP 2019

Section 6

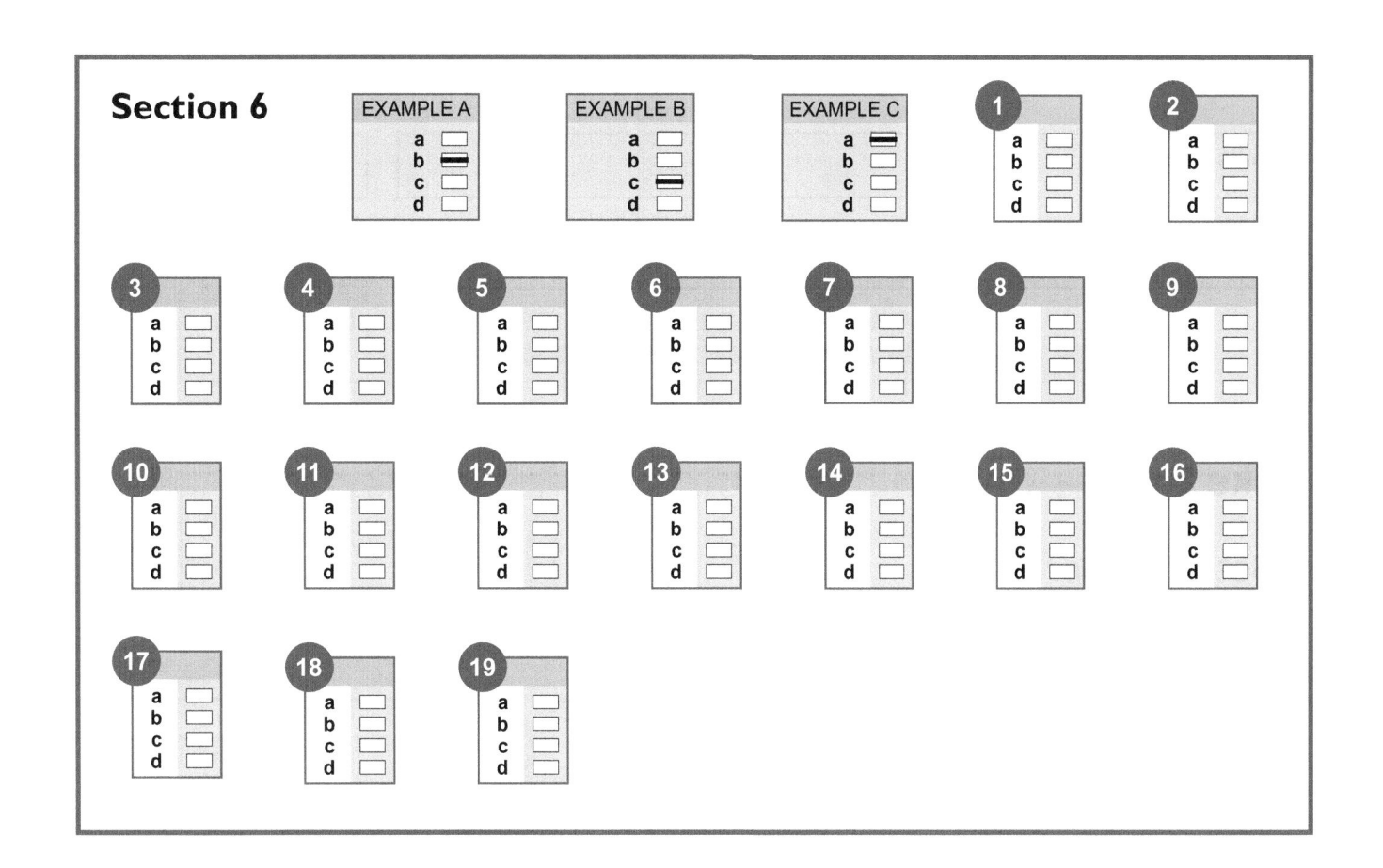

EXAMPLE A: b
EXAMPLE B: c
EXAMPLE C: a

Set B: Paper 2

Pupil's name:

School name:

Test date:

Date of Birth

Please mark like this: ▭

Set B: Paper 2

Section 1

EXAMPLE A
- angry
- cough
- cold ■
- shiver

1
- quicker
- calm
- messy
- delay

2
- perhaps
- definitely
- sometimes
- unlikely

3
- soothe
- stress
- heal
- respect

4
- common
- unnecessary
- awkward
- boring

5
- pull
- shuffle
- throw
- push

6
- strong
- steady
- shaky
- flexible

7
- right
- certain
- wise
- confused

8
- cure
- dislike
- harm
- ruin

9
- teenager
- baby
- human
- parent

10
- shrink
- widen
- ache
- recover

11
- rough
- furry
- spotty
- bald

12
- employ
- manage
- work
- fire

13
- town
- seaside
- countryside
- nation

14
- old
- cheap
- second-hand
- unfashionable

15
- make
- continue
- prevent
- encourage

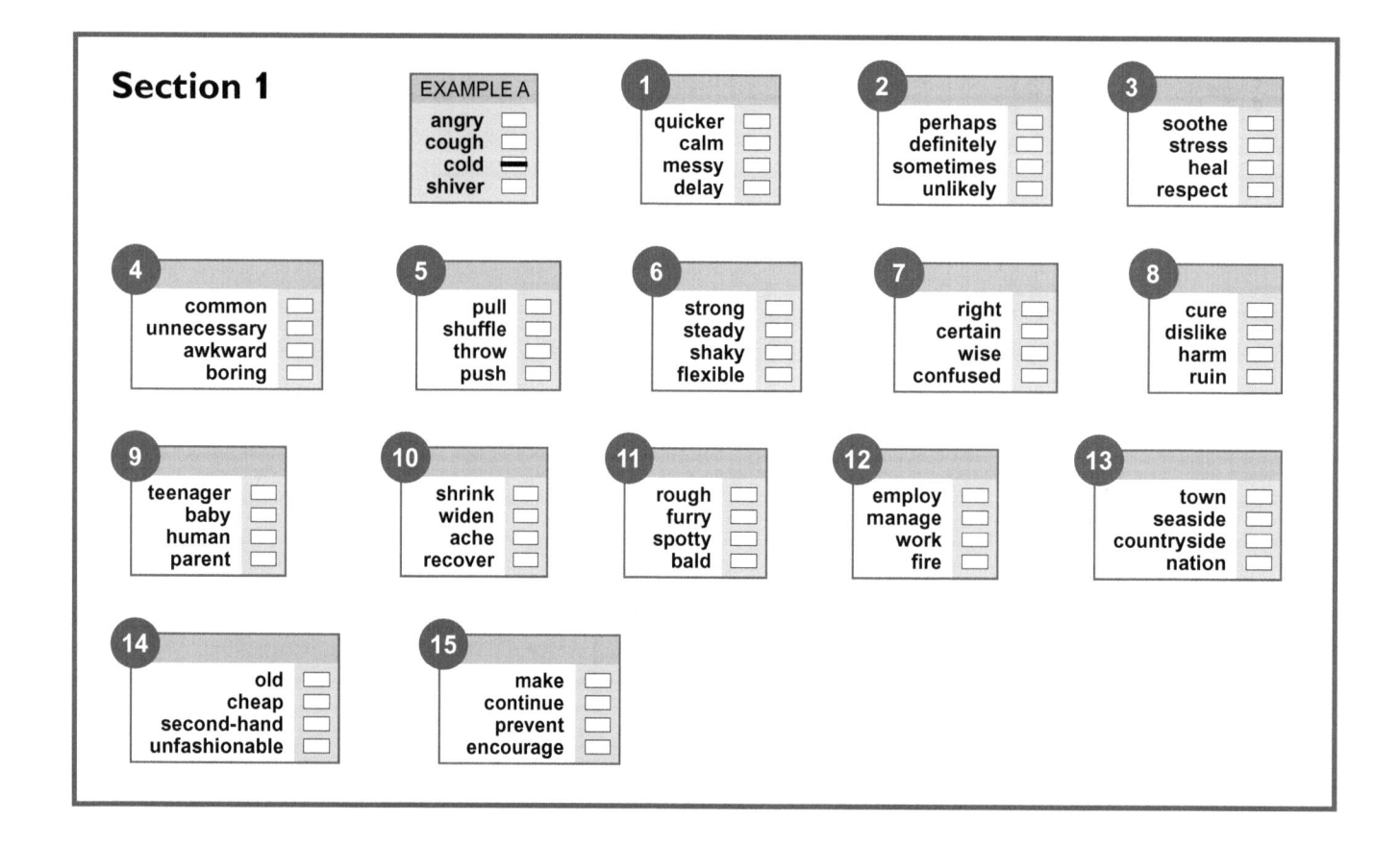

Section 2

Each word has two or more missing letters. Mark the box next to each letter that needs to be added to complete the word.

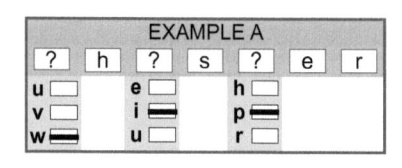

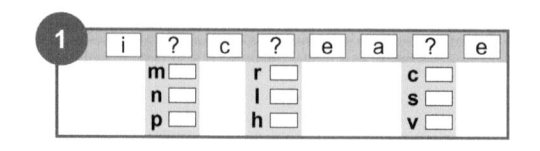

EXAMPLE A
? h ? s ? e r
- u
- v
- w ■
- e
- i ■
- u
- h
- p ■
- r

1
i ? c ? e a ? e
- m
- n
- p
- r
- l
- h
- c
- s
- v

11+ / CEM / 8-9 / Answer Sheets

Section 2 Continued

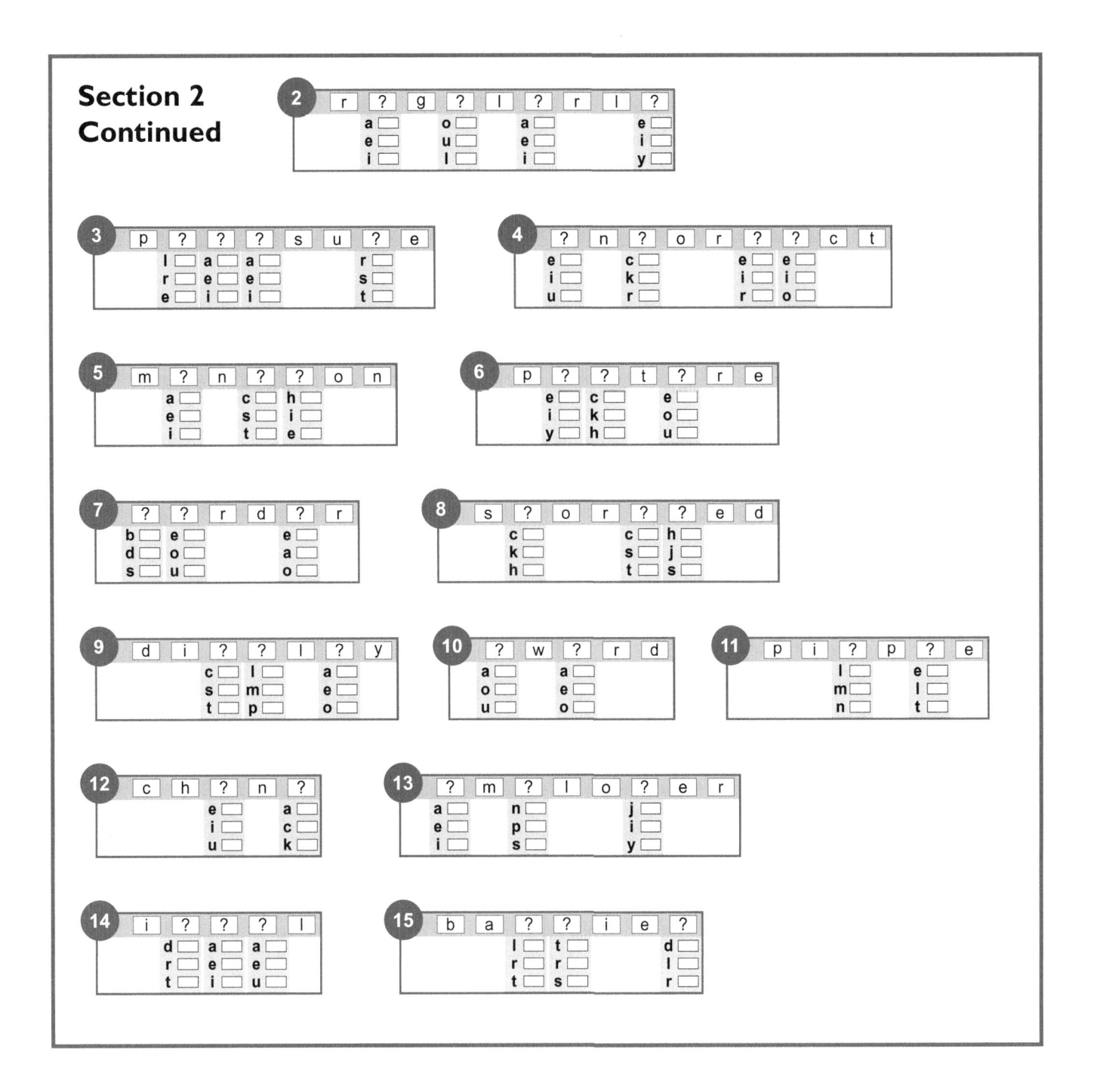

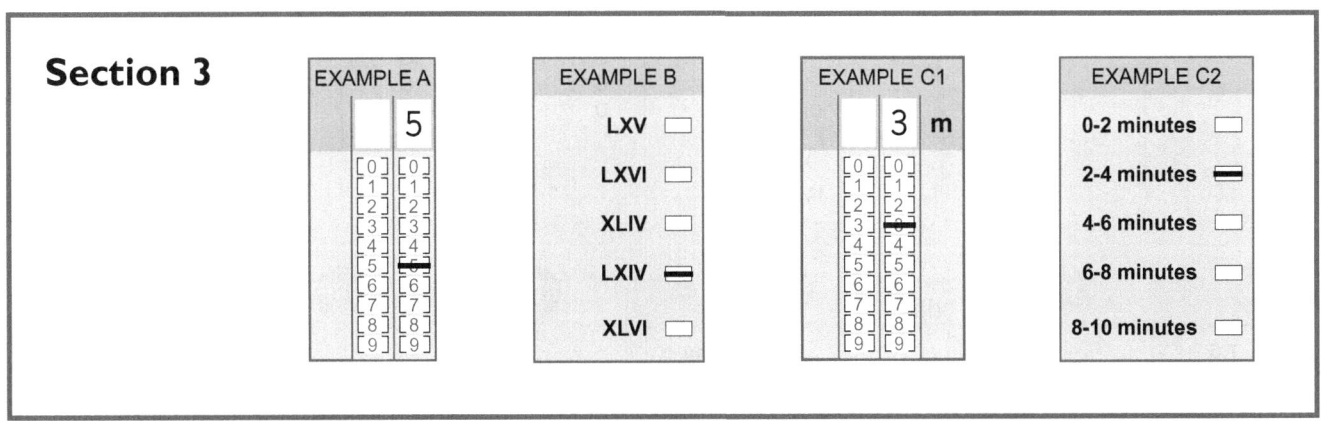

2. r ? g ? l ? r l ?
- a / o / a / e
- e / u / e / i
- i / l / i / y

3. p ? ? ? s u ? e
- l / a / a / r
- r / e / e / s
- e / i / i / t

4. ? n ? o r ? ? c t
- e / c / e / e
- i / k / i / i
- u / r / r / o

5. m ? n ? ? o n
- a / c / h
- e / s / i
- i / t / e

6. p ? ? t ? r e
- e / c / e
- i / k / o
- y / h / u

7. ? ? r d ? r
- b / e / e
- d / o / a
- s / u / o

8. s ? o r ? ? e d
- c / c / h
- k / s / j
- h / t / s

9. d i ? ? l ? y
- c / l / a
- s / m / e
- t / p / o

10. ? w ? r d
- a / a
- o / e
- u / o

11. p i ? p ? e
- l / e
- m / l
- n / t

12. c h ? n ?
- e / a
- i / c
- u / k

13. ? m ? l o ? e r
- a / n / j
- e / p / i
- i / s / y

14. i ? ? ? l
- d / a / a
- r / e / e
- t / i / u

15. b a ? ? i e ?
- l / t / d
- r / r / l
- t / s / r

Section 3

EXAMPLE A: 5

EXAMPLE B: LXIV

EXAMPLE C1: 3 m

EXAMPLE C2: 2-4 minutes

Section 3 Continued

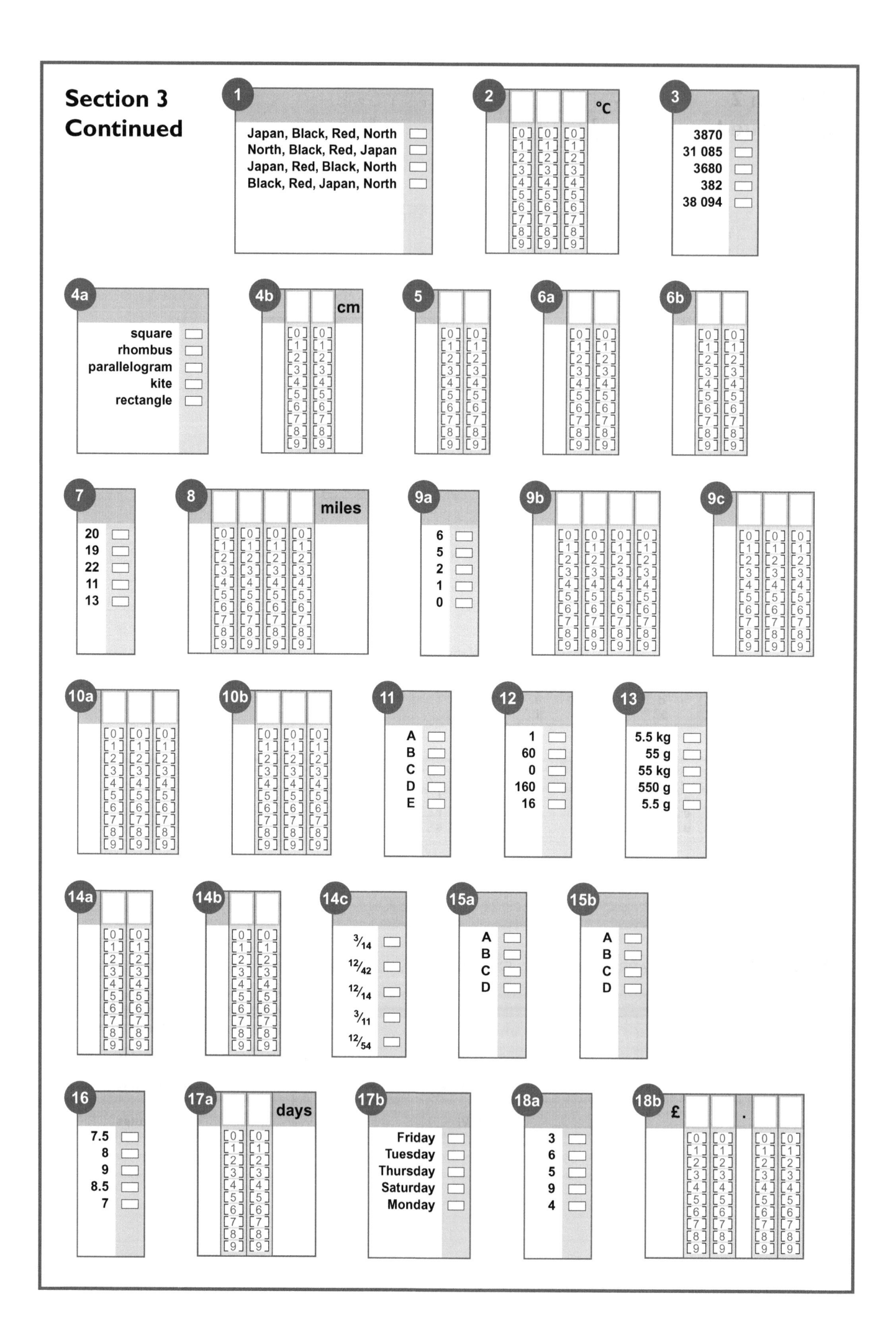

1
- Japan, Black, Red, North
- North, Black, Red, Japan
- Japan, Red, Black, North
- Black, Red, Japan, North

2 °C

3
- 3870
- 31 085
- 3680
- 382
- 38 094

4a
- square
- rhombus
- parallelogram
- kite
- rectangle

4b cm

5

6a

6b

7
- 20
- 19
- 22
- 11
- 13

8 miles

9a
- 6
- 5
- 2
- 1
- 0

9b

9c

10a

10b

11
- A
- B
- C
- D
- E

12
- 1
- 60
- 0
- 160
- 16

13
- 5.5 kg
- 55 g
- 55 kg
- 550 g
- 5.5 g

14a

14b

14c
- 3/14
- 12/42
- 12/14
- 3/11
- 12/54

15a
- A
- B
- C
- D

15b
- A
- B
- C
- D

16
- 7.5
- 8
- 9
- 8.5
- 7

17a days

17b
- Friday
- Tuesday
- Thursday
- Saturday
- Monday

18a
- 3
- 6
- 5
- 9
- 4

18b £ .

Section 3 Continued

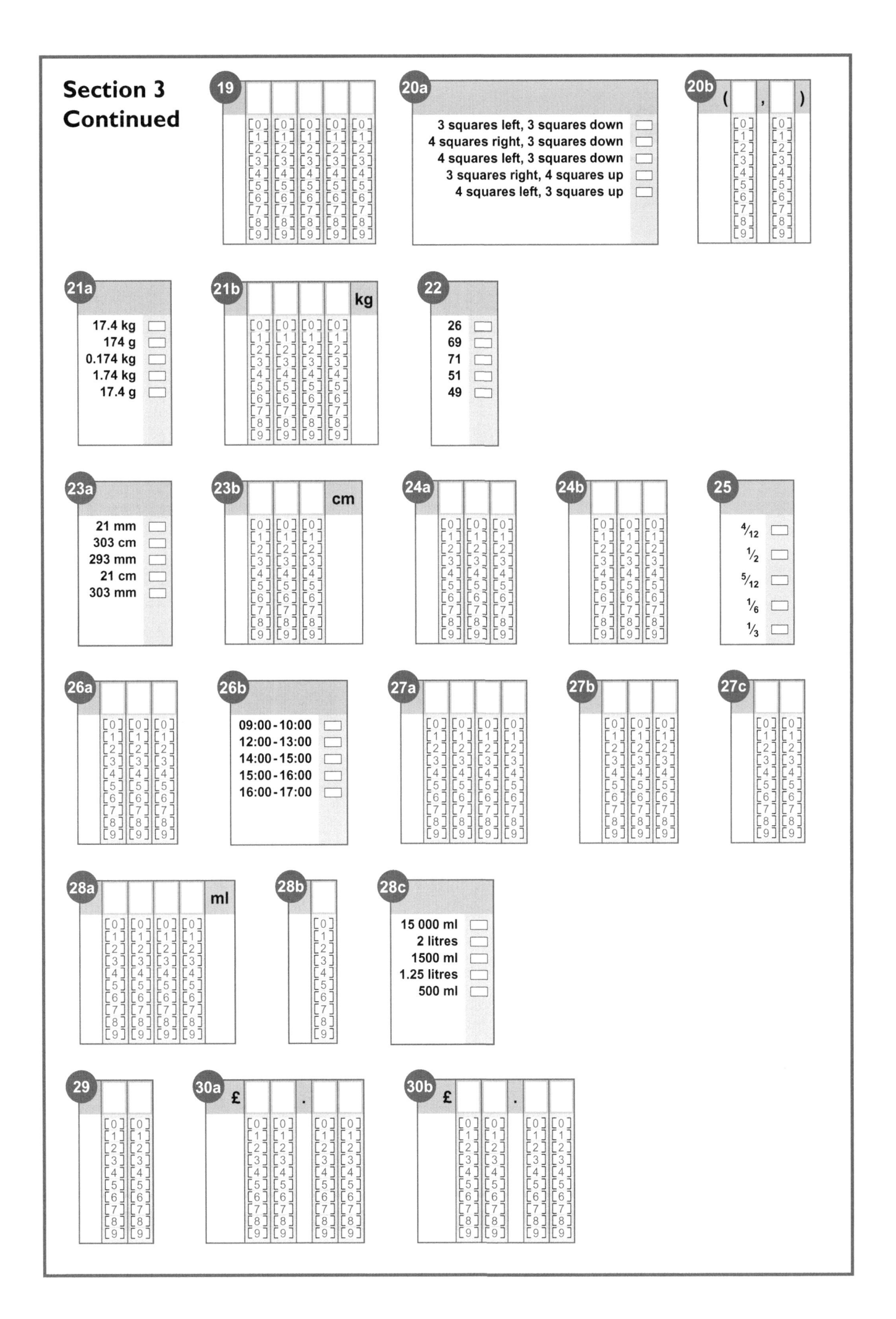

19 [answer grid: 5 digits]

20a
- 3 squares left, 3 squares down ☐
- 4 squares right, 3 squares down ☐
- 4 squares left, 3 squares down ☐
- 3 squares right, 4 squares up ☐
- 4 squares left, 3 squares up ☐

20b ([digit] , [digit])

21a
- 17.4 kg ☐
- 174 g ☐
- 0.174 kg ☐
- 1.74 kg ☐
- 17.4 g ☐

21b [4-digit grid] kg

22
- 26 ☐
- 69 ☐
- 71 ☐
- 51 ☐
- 49 ☐

23a
- 21 mm ☐
- 303 cm ☐
- 293 mm ☐
- 21 cm ☐
- 303 mm ☐

23b [3-digit grid] cm

24a [3-digit grid]

24b [3-digit grid]

25
- 4/12 ☐
- 1/2 ☐
- 5/12 ☐
- 1/6 ☐
- 1/3 ☐

26a [3-digit grid]

26b
- 09:00 – 10:00 ☐
- 12:00 – 13:00 ☐
- 14:00 – 15:00 ☐
- 15:00 – 16:00 ☐
- 16:00 – 17:00 ☐

27a [4-digit grid]

27b [3-digit grid]

27c [2-digit grid]

28a [4-digit grid] ml

28b [1-digit grid]

28c
- 15 000 ml ☐
- 2 litres ☐
- 1500 ml ☐
- 1.25 litres ☐
- 500 ml ☐

29 [2-digit grid]

30a £ [2-digit] . [2-digit]

30b £ [2-digit] . [2-digit]

CGP

11+ Practice Papers

For the **CEM** test

Parents' Guide

Ages 8-9

Published by CGP

Editors:

Andy Cashmore, Emma Clayton, Robbie Driscoll, Alex Fairer, Katherine Faudemer, Zoe Fenwick,
Sam Mann, Tom Miles, Alison Palin, Hannah Roscoe, Sean Walsh, Ruth Wilbourne

With thanks to Alex Fairer, Sharon Keeley-Holden, Holly Robinson and Glenn Rogers for the proofreading.

Please note that CGP is not associated with CEM in any way.
This book does not include any official questions and is not endorsed by CEM.
CEM, Centre for Evaluation and Monitoring, Durham University and *The University of Durham* are all trademarks of The University of Durham.

ISBN: 978 1 78908 246 3

Printed by Elanders Ltd, Newcastle upon Tyne
Clipart from Corel®

Text, design, layout and original illustrations
© Coordination Group Publications Ltd. (CGP) 2019
All rights reserved.

Photocopying more than 5% of a paper is not permitted, even if you have a CLA licence.
Extra copies are available from CGP with next day delivery • 0800 1712 712 • www.cgpbooks.co.uk

What This Pack Contains

What this pack contains

This pack contains **four** 11+ Mixed Practice Papers for the CEM test for ages 8-9.

The questions in these papers have been written to provide age-appropriate practice, with questions written in a similar style to the real exam. They are designed to test your child's Verbal Reasoning, Comprehension, Non-Verbal Reasoning and Maths skills.

Each of the practice papers in this pack has an accompanying **multiple-choice answer sheet**, just like the answer sheets used in the real 11+ exams. There are also **full answers** to every question in the separate **answer booklet**.

You can also download and play the **online audio instructions**, which are similar to the instructions that your child will hear on test day. (Depending on the format of the test in your area, the instructions could be played as an audio recording, like the ones we have provided, or they may be read aloud by an exam invigilator.)

You can find the audio downloads at:

cgpbooks.co.uk/11plustestaudio

This set of papers also includes a **free Online Edition**. For details of how to access your Online Edition, just follow the instructions in the box below:

How to access your free Online Edition

This book includes a free Online Edition to read on your PC, Mac or tablet.
You'll just need to go to **cgpbooks.co.uk/extras** and enter this code:

2488 4148 1927 7535

By the way, this code only works for one person. If somebody else has used this book before you, they might have already claimed the Online Edition.

The pages that follow in this Parents' Guide are designed to give some guidance and information on how to best prepare for the 11+ test, as well as how to support your child in performing as well as they can.

- Before you start, it's important to remember that preparing to take the 11+ can be a stressful time for both parents and pupils. Thinking about ways in which you can minimise the pressure on your child will help to make sure that the process is as positive an experience as possible.
- By using age-appropriate practice to prepare for the 11+ test early, your child can begin to build the skills and confidence they will need to perform well when they eventually take the test.
- The practice papers in this pack allow your child to develop their Verbal Reasoning, Comprehension, Non-Verbal Reasoning and Maths 11+ skills. These skills can have a beneficial impact on your child's whole education, regardless of whether they pass the 11+ test.

What is the 11+?

It can be tricky to find reliable information about the 11+ and how to prepare for it. This page covers the basics — what the 11+ test is and how it works.

The 11+ is a selective test

Most secondary schools in the UK are comprehensive — they're non-selective and accept children of all abilities. But in some areas, selective state secondary schools (grammar schools) still exist. These schools select their pupils based on academic ability.

The 11+ test is used to determine if a child is suitable for grammar school. It's also used for entry to some independent schools. Children usually sit the test in the first term of their last year at primary school.

Some schools select pupils based just on the 11+ test results, but others look at other factors when considering an application, e.g. whether you live close to the school, or if you have other children at the school.

The format of the test varies

The exact format of the 11+ test varies depending on the school or Local Authority (LA) you're applying to, as well as on the provider that sets the test. There are two main test providers for the 11+ — **GL Assessment** and **CEM**. However, in some cases, the test papers will be written by the school, or by a consortium of schools in that area.

Make sure you know which of these providers is responsible for the test in your area, and find out as much information as you can about the format of the test before you start.

Wherever you are, there are four main subjects that can be tested:

> **Verbal Reasoning** — problem-solving and logic using words, letters, numbers, etc.
> **Non-Verbal Reasoning** — problem-solving and logic using pictures and symbols.
> **Maths** — often at the same level as the SATs, but it may be more challenging.
> **English** — reading comprehension, grammar and sometimes a writing task.

Tests set by GL Assessment can include any combination of these four subjects (you won't necessarily have to do all four). Traditionally, there would be a different test paper for each subject — however, some GL regions now have mixed papers, with two papers that each cover more than one subject. Check the format of the test in your region well in advance of test day.

Papers set by CEM are usually mixed, and will cover Verbal Reasoning, Non-Verbal Reasoning and Maths. However, CEM Verbal Reasoning does contain some of the same elements as GL English, such as comprehension.

The tests are usually either **multiple choice** (MC) or **standard answer** (SA) format.

> **Multiple choice** — there's a separate answer sheet. There's usually a choice of five options for each answer, and the answers may be computer-marked.
> **Standard answer** — there are spaces on the question paper for the pupil to write their own answers. There will usually not be any answer options given for the pupil to choose from.

Using the Practice Papers

This advice will help you to get the most out of this set of practice papers. You can tailor the way you use these papers to suit your child and the level they are working at.

These practice papers can be taken in multiple-choice format

There is advice on filling in the multiple-choice answer sheets on page 3 of the answer sheet booklet. Read through this advice with your child before you begin. Make sure that they understand what they need to do before they begin a paper, and that they are filling in the answer sheet which matches the paper they are attempting.

How to set the practice papers

Do the practice papers at a time when your child usually works well. This will help them work to the best of their ability. Your child should attempt the practice paper at a clear table in a quiet area, free from distractions and interruptions. They'll need a sharp pencil, an eraser and a pencil sharpener.

As the real 11+ exams may be a while off, you might want to start by helping your child to build their confidence and become familiar with the test. You could do this by:

- Taking these practice papers as an 'open-book' test. This means that, rather than sitting the papers under exam conditions, your child has access to other 11+ study materials that can help them.
- Ignoring the time limit. This will mean your child is able to concentrate on question content, without the pressure of performing under timed conditions.

Once your child feels more confident with the test style and format, you could ask them to complete a paper in test conditions.

If you do want to mimic real exam conditions, you can play the online audio content. The audio runs through the instructions found on the front of the practice paper, and will give your child information about the timings for each section. If you're not using the online audio instructions, you could read out the instructions on the front of the practice paper before your child begins, and monitor the time they are allowed for each section. Make sure that they understand what they have to do. It may help to position your child so they can see a watch or clock to help them keep track of the time they have left.

Encourage them to read over their answers if they finish within the time limit, but don't give them extra time to do this. Mark their test using the answers in the separate answer booklet.

Marking the practice papers

You should give one mark for each correct answer your child gave within the time limit, then work out the total score. There's no set pass mark for the 11+ — it will vary from school to school and year to year. However, for these practice papers, we suggest that your child aims for a score of 85% or more. If your child consistently achieves this target within the time allowed, they may be ready to try one of the practice paper packs for ages 9-10.

If they score below 85%, looking at your child's score can help you determine areas that your child struggles with. For example, if your child scored 60%, got to the end, but got 40% of the questions wrong, they need to brush up on their accuracy. If they scored 60%, got nearly all the questions right, but didn't finish the test, they need to work faster. There is further guidance on these areas on page 6.

Don't worry if your child struggles initially — the 11+ is intended to be challenging, and some of the questions will be quite different to what your child has seen before at school. The benefit of starting 11+ preparation early is that it gives plenty of time to build up their knowledge, skills and experience to be able to tackle the exams with confidence.

Improving Your Child's Score

For your child to do well in their 11+, they'll need to work quickly and avoid making mistakes. Here's some advice to help improve your child's score and test technique.

Improving accuracy

When your child is just starting out, it's a good idea to focus on their accuracy and understanding, rather than speed. You can work on their speed when they're a bit more confident.

Once your child has finished a paper and you've marked it, you should work through the questions they got wrong together, using the solutions in the answer book. That way, they will know how they should have answered those questions, and can use this knowledge when approaching similar questions in the future.

If there are particular skills or topics that your child is consistently answering incorrectly (for example, cloze questions or multiplication questions), then you can target these areas with extra practice.

Once your child has begun to improve on those weaker areas, you can keep coming back to them at regular intervals to make sure they can still get them right.

Improving speed

In the real 11+ test, children are deliberately put under time pressure. This helps schools distinguish between good candidates and the best ones. Once your child can accurately answer 11+ questions, use these tips to help them improve their speed:

- Encourage your child only to check their answers if they have time at the end of the test.
- You could introduce games to get them working faster — try using a stopwatch to time a set of questions, and encourage your child to 'beat the clock' by finishing before the time runs out.
- For comprehension questions, it's important that your child can read the text quickly. Encouraging them to read aloud at home will help provide an indicator of your child's fluency.

As your child builds up their speed, make sure they don't forget about accuracy. Working quickly can introduce the risk of making silly mistakes, such as not reading the question properly, missing a key piece of information, or recording the answer incorrectly.

Working on test technique

Your child will score better on the 11+ if they improve their test technique. Good test technique is also important for their SATs, and other exams later in their education. When they start working through assessment papers, remind them to do the following things:

- Read the front of the paper and enter the correct information on the answer sheets provided.
- Skip any questions that are really difficult, or which are taking a long time — they can come back to them if there's time at the end.
- If they can't do a question and they're running out of time, make a sensible guess. For multiple-choice questions, they may be able to rule out one or two options that definitely aren't correct, which gives a better chance of guessing which of the remaining options is right.

If your child's test is in multiple-choice format, there are some other specific techniques to practise:

- Marking the correct box neatly and quickly using a horizontal line.
- Making sure they mark the answer in the correct box, especially if they skip a question.
- If they don't finish the paper, filling in the rest of the answers randomly.

It's a good idea to practise good exam technique and get your child used to working in test conditions. That way, your child will be well prepared when the time comes to sit the real exam.

How to Approach the Test

As well as making sure your child can answer 11+ questions quickly and accurately, you should also focus on your approach to the test itself. By encouraging your child to see the 11+ positively, you can help them to approach the test in a way that will maximise their chances of scoring highly.

Staying positive

If you're starting to prepare your child for the 11+ early, the test can seem a long way off. Preparation for the test can be stressful, so it's important to try to make your child's experience a positive one.

When doing practice papers, any low scores should be approached with a positive attitude. You could encourage your child to view them as an opportunity to pinpoint any strengths and weaknesses, otherwise it'll be easy for them to focus on the negatives. Areas for improvement can then be targeted in order to do better next time.

Rewarding your child for their hard work can help to keep them motivated. Positively reinforcing the effort they are putting in will encourage them to persevere with their test preparation.

Planning your approach

Ideally, your child should be working at 11+ standard well before they sit the test. Consider when they might be ready to attempt some questions levelled for 10-11 standard — it may be useful to create a timeline so that you can plan how your child can build their skills throughout their preparation.

You could use a star chart to reward your child's progress. This could help them to keep track of how well they are doing, as well as helping to keep them motivated.

If your child struggles with the practice materials in this pack, they may need to use materials targeted at a lower age range. The age ranges stated on practice materials give some guidance on their difficulty level. Older children can still benefit from using 7-8 resources if they need to develop their skills. Equally, if your child finds the materials targeted at their age range too easy, they may be ready to try materials aimed at a slightly higher level.

Fun ways to improve

It's important that 11+ practice doesn't start to feel like a chore, especially if your child is beginning to prepare for the test early. There are lots of activities and games that you can use to help your child continue to develop skills they will need for the 11+. These might include:

- Completing puzzles such as tangrams. This will help them to develop their spatial awareness.
- Reading a variety of fiction and non-fiction texts. This will help your child become familiar with different writing styles and build up a wide vocabulary.
- Playing word games or crosswords in puzzle books or on the internet.
- Writing stories, letters to friends or newspaper articles inspired by interesting headlines.
- Practising number puzzles such as Kakuro. This will help to develop your child's maths skills.

The right school for your child

If your child is really struggling with 11+ preparation, it might be worth considering whether or not your child is suited to grammar school. Sitting the 11+ is a choice and you can withdraw your child from the process at any point if you decide grammar school might not be for them.

Speak to your child and find out their opinions. They may have concerns about grammar school that you can talk to them about. A grammar school environment does not suit every learner — remember that there are many excellent comprehensive schools where your child can be happy and successful.